INTELLECTUAL DISABILITY
THE RESPONSE OF THE CHURCH

Edited by

Brian Kelly and Patrick McGinley

Lisieux Hall P

INTELLECTUAL DISABILITY
THE RESPONSE OF THE CHURCH

Published by:

Lisieux Hall Publications, Whittle-le-Woods, Chorley, Lancashire, England PR6 7DX

Copyright © The Brothers of Charity, 2000

A catalogue entry for this book is available from the British Library

ISBN 1-8700335 27 9

The Brothers of Charity and Lisieux Hall Publications are pleased to have this opportunity of publishing Intellectual Disability – Response of the Church as a project marking the celebration of the millennium of the birth of Jesus Christ.

INTELLECTUAL DISABILITY
THE RESPONSE OF THE CHURCH

Edited by

Brian Kelly and Patrick McGinley

Brothers of Charity, Lisieux Hall, Whittle-le-Woods, Chorley, Lancashire, England. PR6 7DX

Recent Publications available from Lisieux Hall

Innovations in Advocacy and Empowerment, *edited by Linda Ward.*
Ward has created a truly universal and valuable resource; informative and accessible for clients, professionals and carers alike. Mental Health Care.

Innovations in Health Care for People with Intellectual Disabilities,
edited by Michael Kerr.
Presents an up-to-date review of best practice in the delivery of health care and advances in medical science.

Innovations in Evaluating Services for People with Intellectual Disabilities, edited by Roy McConkey.
The international authorship make this one of the most comprehensive and up-to-date reviews on current thinking about service evaluation. Essential reading for planners and managers.

Innovations in Family Support for People with Learning Disabilities,
edited by Peter and Helle Mittler.
This book is a must for all professionals working in the field. It will become a key reference volume in the area of family studies. Frontline

Innovations in Educating Communities about Learning Disabilities,
edited by Roy McConkey.
Two features distinguish this addition to the campaigning literature; the selection of often telling cartoons and the emphasis on supporting people with disability labels to be their own ambassadors. Care Weekly

Innovations in Educating Children with Severe Learning Disabilities,
edited by John Harris.
It is rare to read a book about the national curriculum and children with severe learning disabilities that is readable and practical. But this is one such book.
Care Weekly

Innovations in Employment Training and Work for People with Learning Difficulties, edited by Roy McConkey & Patrick McGinley.
Useful practical guide to a number of innovative programmes in vocational training and employment in the UK and other countries.
Mental Handicap Research

INTELLECTUAL DISABILITY
THE RESPONSE OF THE CHURCH

Contents

Chapter	Title	Page

Foreword
by the Archbishop of Liverpool

The disciples of the Lord Jesus bring these convictions for those with special needs. They are convinced that the Charity, that is the love and concern, which is the Charity, love and concern of God our Father is poured into our hearts by the Holy Spirit. Brothers of Charity accept the challenge to allow everything they say and do to be formed, shaped, determined by nothing less than the respect, the understanding, the passions which is of God.

It is the same spirit which drives on the enterprises described in the following pages.

But the word 'Lisieux' sets before us another challenge. The gift of God received through Saint Therese of Lisieux, includes an ever deeper awareness of the conviction of Saint Paul: it is the weakest members in the Body of Christ, which is the Church, which are indispensable. Every member needs and is needed, every member gives and receives.

This project of the Brothers of Charity and Lisieux Hall, is fitting for the year 2000, to celebrate Christ, yesterday, today, for ever.

With my best wishes,

Yours sincerely,

+ Patrick Kelly

Archbishop of Liverpool

1 CHANGING TIMES
AN INTRODUCTION AND OVERVIEW

Brian Kelly and Patrick McGinley

Over the past twenty-five years there has been a radical change in the way that society views disability. The Church has been both profoundly affected by and has contributed significantly to, the manner in which our society has sought to move from segregation to integration, and from marginalisation to inclusion in relation to people with disabilities.

The position of disabled people in Society and in the Church and has always been a precarious one. Discrimination has been deep-rooted. The person with a disability was most likely to be viewed as a 'holy innocent' or an 'object of charity' with nothing much to offer the rest of us. We are now just beginning to recognise the gifts and contributions that people with disabilities can and will make to society and to the Church provided that we are open to them, that we recognise their uniqueness and respect their individuality.

Throughout its history the Church has sought to alleviate the suffering of disabled people in one form or another. The manner of doing this has sometimes been misguided, leading to segregation, marginalisation, isolation, discrimination, and ultimately even to abuse. More often than not the paternalistic nature of the Church was reflected in the way people were treated which was often harsh.

As our society has changed so has the Church. In many respects, but not all, the hierarchical and clerically dominated Church with its emphasis on sacramental observance has given way to a Church which is more in tune with the needs of people as individuals. The Church that was once the protector of doctrine has given way to a Church concerned about the interaction of people in community, the protection of the most vulnerable, and now recognises that contribution which can be made by so many people including those with a disability.

Today we are challenged by people with intellectual disability. They are no longer satisfied with being the recipients of our charity. They are demanding to be heard, to play an equal part in our communities. The Church, although sometimes slow in recognising and responding to the challenge, is beginning to change. This book, which builds on our earlier volume *Mental Handicap – Challenge to the Church* (1990), illustrates what is being carried out at a grass roots level by Church communities in different parts of the world. It shows what can be done when people reflect more deeply about what it means to be human, what it means to have a disability, what it means to be Church.

A fundamental journey of understanding is spelled out clearly by Fr. Frank Daly in his chapter **A Man Came...** Describing his work with 'John' whom he met in a back street off-licence, Frank takes us on a personal journey cleverly interweaving three strands – his relationship and work with John; the deepening of Frank's personal understanding of what is at the heart of working with people with a disability; and the changing thrust of the work of the Church with those of us who may have a disability. The 'grounding' of Frank's personal journey, in the journey of the Church in his month-by-month work with John, makes the radical shift in his own thinking and in Church work easily accessible as it leads us in a way, which is both simple and profound, to an understanding of the radical transformations involved. Frank sees himself initially as John's helper, and he moves gradually from that to seeing his work in terms of establishing the right of people with disabilities to be part of the wider community; and develops through Frank's deepening appreciation that, ' *The Liturgy was not simply to be celebrated with and for our friends, but also by them for others'* to an appreciation of the real worth and the deep significance of people like John who show us, *'where our values have been misplaced, where the soul of society has been lost, and our whole sense of direction misguided'*; Frank concludes his personal spiritual journey with John with the profound conclusion,

'The 'witness' for the Light would speak to us, show us the way, 'contribute' to our lives and the true richness we need, if only we will let him speak, and listen to him.'

Fr. Paul Wadell's searching chapter on **Access to the Sacraments** interweaves the themes of the fundamental entitlement of people with a disability to full sacramental participation with the deepening of our own understanding and appreciation of the central role of the sacraments in all of our lives. Paul argues that the greatest injustice inflicted on persons with disabilities, *'is to exclude them not for their sake but for ours. We keep them at a distance because we do not want to see that we too are helpless and needy ...'.* He goes on to explore Jesus, as sacrament, perfectly human because of *'the ability to rest in his neediness and find power in his incompleteness.'* He argues that it is not for us to explain or define the sacraments – that is what God does for us in Christ whose saving activity defines the substance of the sacraments, concluding that questions about who should receive them can't be related to our sense of what is right or appropriate but only by discerning the over-riding intention of God – *'We are owed access to God because God desires to be accessible to us. The sacraments articulate how much God wants to be part of our lives.'*

In his chapter, **Shared Learning in Communities, Congregations and Churches**, Roy McConkey explores three issues, namely,

1.   the influences which predispose people to reject people with disabilities and how these can be overcome;

2.   the contributions which Christian communities can make to the social and community life of a person with a learning disability and what local congregations require to do to make this happen; and

3.   how social relationships with people who have an intellectual disability can underpin one's Christianity and the relevance of this for our forms of worship and Christian education.

Roy concludes that the very presence of a person with a disability in our community, keeps alive *'the fruits of the spirit of which Paul wrote.'* In this respect, *'Modern society more than ever, needs people with disabilities to remind them of what it means to be human.'*

Mary Therese Harrington's chapter on Catechesis, **Affectivity and Symbol in the Process of Catechesis**, explains the difference between faith and education (our awakening to the mystery that we are loved by a merciful God), and the simple transmission of knowledge. Mary Therese defines affectivity as the ability *'to feel and express emotions. It is different from intelligence and will, but just as fundamental to the well-being of a person.'* Our understanding and the way she invites us into her appreciation of the importance of affectivity in catechesis makes an important contribution and, at the same time, demands a significant shift in traditional thinking about catechesis. She says, *'It includes the scents of flowers, of warm bread, of cocoa. It includes the light and warmth in a room...* (but, affectivity in catechesis) *is disciplined and demanding. It has tensions, conflicts, reconciliations and break-throughs.'.* Mary Therese's treatment of symbolic awareness makes a particular contribution to the place of symbol in catechesis. She argues that symbolic activity means having a double vision, maintaining contact with the 'here and now' phenomenon and a 'beyond' phenomenon – *'one must keep* (these visions) *in tension and in balance; sad things can happen if this balance is lost.'* Sadly, too often the balance is lost and Mary Therese's chapter makes a substantial contribution to recovering that important sense of symbol.

Fr. David Wilson's contribution on **l'Arche** is unique indeed, written as it is, in the form of an inspirational poem. We are introduced to the profound thinking and to the humanity and theology represented by l'Arche through being led on a journey through a full day in a l'Arche community. We are introduced to Hubert, Jeanne, Mariethe, Marie-Giles, Odile, Jean, and Frances. We are drawn in to the house overlooking the white-capped sea and to the community life, full and caring, filled with prayer and liturgy, touched by past woundedness and hurt, and yet illustrating a humble confidence of peace, understanding, and presence – *'Yes, community life is not easy. "Come spirit of Jesus, enable us to live in your way".'*

In ***Celebrating the Eucharist with People with a Learning Difficulty***, Axel Liégeois gives us a detailed and in-depth analysis of celebrating the Eucharist with people who have learning difficulties in Flanders. He leads us through the Celebration picking out a lively interaction between the Eucharistic tradition on the one hand, and the *'possibilities and life circumstances'* of people with a learning difficulty on the other hand. We are led through the rich symbolism, the liturgy of the word, the breaking of the bread, the sharing of the cup, in a spirit of prayerfulness and openness and with an emphasis on Celebration.

Claude Madec describes his work in establishing a pastoral care service in the West of Ireland. Identifying the principal function of the Pastoral Care Programme, as offering support within the services in the area of human and spiritual development at a personal and community level, Claude lays down a theoretical framework including elements like promoting awareness and understanding of pastoral care; nurturing spiritual development; nurturing personal development; nurturing community development; and contributing to nurturing 'ethos' within a local service. But Claude goes much further than this by giving us a detailed account of the practical application of these principles taking us through celebration and liturgy, workshops on community and liturgy, retreats and times of renewal, parents' days of renewal, pilgrimages to the ancient abbey of Ballintubber to climbing Co. Mayo's sacred mountain, Croagh Patrick. Happily, Claude gives a wealth of detail, the difficulties together with the joys, and he does so in an inviting manner. Readers will very likely find practical projects clearly described here which can be followed and built upon by those working in pastoral care or interested in developing a pastoral care service anywhere.

In ***Circles of Support*** Mandy Neville and Barry McIver describe a social organization known as a Circle of Support designed to combat isolation and loneliness in people with a disability. Mandy and Barry start by placing the idea of Circles of Support in its historical context, from its United States origins, through a national conference in Bristol in 1992, to the present time. Using a social model of disability, we learn that the support circles provide a catalyst and a conduit for people who feel isolated and excluded through difference, to find a place in the community at large, and we are introduced to an exciting view of the concept of inclusion ... *'based on a paradigm shift, a cultural* *change which is underpinned by the belief that all people, however labelled, have the right to participate and belong in communities.'* We are given practical insights by way of snapshots of Circles in progress, and invited to address some issues and challenges for the Support Circles. We are shown Circles as being the antithesis of isolation, a space and a place, which encourages risk-taking, as persons with a learning difficulty move from isolation to inclusion. *Circles Network,* formed in 1993, is a charity designed with an educational objective to develop and sustain Circles of Support, to offer consultancy and training, and to co-ordinate a range of courses and conferences with a focus on inclusion and serving anyone experiencing exclusion, whether through learning or mental health difficulties, physical or sensory impairment, or enduring ill health.

Julia Granger describes pastoral support work in the dioceses of Arandell and Brighton in her chapter, **We Are One People**. We are given a description of the setting up of a parish network with at least one person from each of 120 parishes – not a professional support structure, something more personal and organic, something more fundamentally linked to the life and work and the people in each individual parish. There is a great emphasis on training and skills development, and great emphasis given to identifying the importance of even small successes as clergy are encouraged to consider more accessible liturgies and parishes change to make our Church more accessible and inclusive for those who may formerly have been marginalised or who may have felt excluded. Developments from the parish network are described, including an integrated drama group, which enhanced the introduction of dance and drama in prayer and liturgy; and a conference for Christians, an interdenominational day where self-advocates worked to clarify their own views of their own participation in church – *'They wanted to be involved and to contribute to the life of their Church.'* Relationships and having friends for this group, as for any group, emerged as a consistent theme just as the range of delegates' likes and dislikes reflected the likes and dislikes of any mixed group of a similar age group. Julia concludes that building true community in our Churches is a life-long task and sees her experience in pastoral care in Arandel and Brighton as a voyage of discovery of unused gifts, of opportunities, of mechanisms for growing community together as *'we are slowly and with difficulty, learning to listen to one another.'*

Using a familiar scriptural image, Agnes Nelson traces the work of **SPRED** from its *Seed* in the Archdiocese of Chicago. She describes the *Shoot and Leaves* which develop in time – we are given a practical, work-a-day story about how SPRED reached out to Pauline who was aged seven and has a severe learning difficulty. We are introduced to the place of liturgical mime, experiences of beauty beyond logic, of pre-conceptual experience, communication through gesture and movement as, *'God transcends senses and intellect, coming close in this act of beauty.'* We are introduced to the *Fruit* of many years of work of SPRED in the Archdiocese emphasizing the seed-bearing nature of the fruit. We have a description of the validation of a certificate course eventually upgraded to a SPRED Diploma as the work of SPRED moves onwards and outwards to other dioceses and downwards to local parishes. Finally, the metaphor would not be complete without *Stones*, the obstacles. Agnes concludes, *'In the Archdiocese of Glasgow the seed of SPRED has been planted and watered, but it is God who provides the growth, the challenge… is to be a people of faith… a people who recognize their incompleteness. The Lord will effect the miracle.*

In the final chapter, Bob Brooke describes the ***Faith and Light Community*** at Seacroft, a council estate in Leeds. Bob introduces us to the regular monthly meetings of Faith and Light – a lively sense of innovation here. He gives us a brief but instructive account of the development of Faith and Light over the years with an emphasis on Internationalism and Ecumenism. The story of how Faith and Light began (a French couple Camille and Gerard with their two sons Loic and Thaddee, who faced a challenge around making a pilgrimage to Lourdes) and how Faith and Light spread all over the world *'Many people who perhaps have experienced rejection or have a low opinion of themselves because of what the world at large says about them, have found in their Faith and Light community a place where they know they are accepted and loved and where they can be themselves and grow in confidence, in self-acceptance, and self-esteem.'*

Conclusion

There are many innovative and exciting projects at various stages of development that cannot be mentioned in this book. These projects are the result of a responsive and increasingly decentralized Church. People with disabilities are now more likely to be participants and organizers of church activities, and are less likely to be casual observers of what goes on. At the beginning of this new Millennium it is the thrust and vitality of projects like these which genuinely embody the Response of the Church.

Biographical Notes

Brian Kelly was born in Scotland and educated at Upholland College, Lancashire, and the Liverpool Institute of Higher Education in Liverpool, where he obtained his BA (Hons) degree in 1984. He has worked for the Brothers of Charity Services in Lancashire since 1985, and was appointed Director of Services in 1999.

From Ballinasloe, Co. Galway, **Patrick McGinley** was trained as a teacher at Christ's College, Liverpool and as a psychologist at the University of Calgary, Alberta, Canada. A fellow of the Psychological Society of Ireland, Patrick has edited several books and published a significant number of professional articles. Prior to being appointed as Director of Services for the Galway Region of the Brothers of Charity, he was Director of Psychology in the same service.

2 'A Man Came...'

Frank Daly

"A man came, sent by God; his name was John. He came as a witness for the light... He was not the light, only a witness to speak for the light..." (John 1: 6-7, 9).

I found 'John' in a back street off-licence in the east end of Nottingham on a dark evening in the autumn of 1978. He had been out only a handful of times in his 27 years because his mother was embarrassed and even a little afraid. She was afraid because he was 'handicapped' - brain damaged shortly after birth, and left with a permanent physical and mental impairment. What would people think of him, of his tantrums, violence and his unpredictable behaviour? So she kept him there, in his home - safe and apart, out of harm's way, out of the way altogether. He was her problem, her 'cross', and she would look after him, she and his Dad. She didn't, couldn't contemplate what might become of him if anything happened to either of them. No, he would 'go' first - she was sure of that - so she would look after him until he did.

John's story is like that of so many others in those days and before - people kept apart, because they were an embarrassment to their families. They were 'handicapped' - a 'handicap' to themselves, to their families and to others. They were 'retarded', 'disabled', 'disadvantaged' or whatever word could be used to describe people who were 'different' from the rest of us, somehow, not the 'full shilling', if indeed we did them the honour of thinking of them as 'people' at all. Not only did they have to contend with the limitations of their condition, but also the wholesale ignorance, even prejudice of the rest of society, which thought that, 'out of sight is out of mind.'

The story of John is also the story of the work of many people, professional and voluntary, to give him the dignity of being a person, an individual - maybe a little slow, a bit jumbled up, a little lacking in the niceties of behaviour - but an individual nevertheless, not one of God's 'little mistakes'.

It is not that long ago, however, that people like John had many problems to contend with that were caused by the ignorance of the rest of society. The famous disabled writer, Louis Battye, expressed this situation very movingly in his paper, *The Chatterley Syndrome.*

> *The cripple is an object of Christian charity, a socio-medical problem, a stumbling nuisance, an embarrassment to the girls he falls in love with. He is a vocation for saints, a livelihood for the manufacturers of wheelchairs, a target for busy-bodies, a means by which prosperous citizens assuage their consciences. He is at the mercy of overworked doctors and nurses, and under-worked bureaucrats and social investigators. He is pitied, ignored, helped and patronised, misunderstood and stared at. But he is hardly ever taken seriously as a man* (Battye, 1976).

They were kept 'out of the way' - either at home, or in the large institutions geared to containment rather than stimulation. Limited objectives and limited expectations were placed upon them, and thus they had a 'good life', so we thought - but what did we know? What did we care as long as they were nowhere near us? They were rarely treated as 'persons', who should have choices, individuals, with gifts of their own to share - they were lumped together as 'handicapped' or 'disadvantaged' people - and no one took the trouble to try to communicate with those who found it difficult to speak, no one thought that here there might be a normal brain functioning and frustrated because it was not taken seriously. We cannot ever fully know just how terrible this must have felt for many people with disabilities or impairing conditions. In 1987, a young Irish man, Christopher Nolan, cerebral palsied from birth, unable to communicate, save with his mother cupping his head so that he could meticulously type every single letter with a stick attached to his head, broke forever the assumptions that able-bodied people have about those with handicapping conditions.

His book, *Under the Eye of the Clock*, is the most revealing I have ever come across about precisely how a person whose body is physically impaired, and who has no speech, feels when he is not taken seriously as a person.

> *Can I climb man-made mountains... Can I mount socially-constructed barriers? Can I ask my family to back me when I know something more than they... What can a speechless crippled boy do?... My handicap curtails my collective conscience, obliterates my voice, beckons ridicule of my smile, and damns my chances of being accepted as normal...*

> *Will they be able to gauge my terrible struggle... can any sane able-bodied person sense how it feels to have evil-intentioned limbs constantly making a mockery of you... how can they hear your cry for life... Can I... crippled as I am, spearhead a new drive to highlight the communicative needs of tongue-tied but normal notioned man? (Nolan, 1987).*

This was the climate in which John, and many people like him, existed. While we can now criticise these attitudes, having become a little 'wiser after the event', we need to humbly admit that the church community is not exempt from ignorance or criticism. For many parents whose children were born with a physical or mental handicap, there were (and are still) a considerable number of burdens to bear, not least the feeling of being rejected by God. In the past, parents would conduct vehement campaigns in order for their children to be 'allowed' to receive Holy Communion. They were more than often met with thinly veiled rebuffs from priests more concerned with canonical exactitude than pastoral care. They were told that this could not be because their children did not 'understand' what Holy Communion was. In one dreadful case, a loving mother who nursed her son for 29 years to his death, was told that, 'It would be like giving it to a dog.' What priests and pastoral workers failed to see was that for these parents, the welcome to Holy Communion meant much more than simply receiving Our Lord. For them it was the symbol that the Church, and Almighty God, welcomed their child as a person, a human being. Our failure to understand this caused much hurt and sadness, which some families have still not got over.

This situation was worsened by what you might call the 'Lourdes mentality'— the opinion that all we needed to do for our children and people with disabilities was to take them to Lourdes. Perhaps they could be cured, perhaps they could become 'normal'. To raise money for this purpose in the pubs and clubs of our cities was never a problem; to bring our friends with a disability into those pubs and clubs was far more difficult. To get people to see that there was nothing wrong with their condition, that it did not need to be 'cured', and that these people wanted desperately to be treated with respect as persons was almost impossible.

So how have things changed and have they changed as much as they might? We must admit that for years many professional people, especially those most intimately involved with disabled people, were doing things that we now take for granted but which, in those days, there was insufficient political will to recognise. Towards the end of the 1960's, the decade of free expression, an upturn in the fortunes of disabled people began to be noticeable. The work of Leonard Cheshire, the war hero, began to spread, and his vision of dignity for people with seriously handicapping conditions began to be adopted. A disabled person, Baroness Masham, took her seat in the House of Lords. The government appointed the first Minister for Disabled People, Mr. Alf Morris MP, and a profoundly deaf man, Jack Ashley was elected to Parliament. The International Year of Disabled People in 1981 did much to draw the attention of everyone to the place people with disabilities wished to occupy in our society - to play a full part in employment, to enjoy accessible facilities for work, worship and leisure.

Within the Church, the French Canadian, Jean Vanier, set up the L'Arche Communities for people with a mental handicap to live together in community not out of the way, but in the midst of towns and villages. The pilgrimage to Lourdes which he organised in 1971, gave birth to the worldwide Faith and Light movement, which has done much to bring people with disabilities into mainstream church and social life, and to support their families. In our own country, pioneering work in Bristol, Liverpool, Westminster and Birmingham, was being done in the religious education of people with learning difficulties and the care of their families.

In our own diocese of Nottingham, the principles for priests and pastoral workers involved with disabled people, were set out in a booklet called '*Guidelines '77*', which was eventually published nationally. We were also responsible for pioneering the idea of a 'Faith and Light Celebration' (as opposed to a 'pilgrimage') - a week of prayer, reflection and spiritual formation for our friends and their families. The first one took place at the Jesuit College of Mount St. Mary, Spinkhill in 1978, and now there are many such events each year all over the world. The widespread practice of using mime and music to interpret the scriptures with and for our friends, also originated in Nottingham. A lot of new ground was broken, a lot of good work was done in those early days, once the floodgates had been opened, and we recognised our responsibilities as the family of the Church to welcome and include those among us with what appeared to be 'limiting' conditions.

So what has happened to our friend, John? Once we found him and gained the trust of his parents, we set up a group with the Sisters of Loreto, for him and thirty people in a similar situation. It began meeting in early 1979 in the convent of Loreto in Nottingham. Fortnightly gatherings took place in which there was a 'theme' for the evening, which was worked out in various ways according to the particular difficulties of each person. A few parents also came along to give mutual support and friendship to each other, and many young people got involved, thus creating an atmosphere where everyone could be regarded as equals with no 'us and them' mentality. The prayer assembly at the end of each meeting was always the highlight, when we brought together our work before the Lord.

Many people like John had not been used to going out, to being with people on a social or a spiritual basis. It was a great delight but also a shock for them. To begin to feel the love and respect of others was a very powerful experience. Often we would have to endure violent opposition and tantrums when it was time to take him home. A scheme of 'Care Days' was begun on the first Monday of each holiday in the home of the Augustinian Fathers of the Assumption, and trips away for a few days or a week at a time began to become a regular part of our lives. On our first holiday away with John, I discovered to my cost that his mother had neglected to tell us that he was frightened of stairs and showers. A bedroom up four flights and the need for at least one shower a day proved to be very interesting!

Once the Loreto Thursday Club became established, it was quickly followed by groups in Loughborough, Scunthorpe, Hinckley, Derby and Leicester, all of which meet regularly, and a number of other groups which meet occasionally. The agency sponsoring them eventually became a registered charity, and all the groups now meet together on at least five occasions every year.

As we came to know John and his friends better, our philosophy towards him changed dramatically. We first of all thought of ourselves as 'helpers', whose job it was to 'help' our friends have a better life, with more opportunities and choices. They were very much on the end of our goodwill and very much dependent on it. Were we simply trying to 'care' for them, to give their parents a break from the strains of looking after them, to bring them into church where they had never been before, so that people would stare at them and make them feel strange? Were we just trying to give them some 'religious education' or 'spiritual formation' as it eventually came to be more realistically called, to tell them something about God and his life which they had not heard before? Well, yes we were, and so many others were doing the same thing.

This was the thrust of our initial work - establishing the right of people with disabilities to be part of the wider community in general, and of the community of the Church in particular, and overcoming the barriers that prevented this from taking place: ignorance, fear and prejudice. This did not happen overnight, indeed we might even say that in some places it has not happened even yet, but progress was definitely made. We had to teach parents not to hone in on the matter of Holy Communion, but to come to see the need for a broader spiritual formation which would certainly include receiving Our Lord.

For the first time, the matter of the sacrament of reconciliation for people with learning difficulties was raised. We came to see that these people often have a more profound sense of sin and the need for forgiveness than we ourselves do. They know when they have hurt someone; they are anxious to make amends and to have their sorrow accepted. The joy of being forgiven by others is a very important thing in their lives; why should the joy of being forgiven by God not also be? To write them off as 'little angels' who don't 'need to go to confession' is patronising in the extreme, and makes all sorts of assumptions about them. If we were serious about giving our friends dignity and self-respect before God, then they should be afforded all the opportunities within the spiritual life that we take for granted as part of our own.

However, the time came when we realised that even this was not enough. The more progress we seemed to make with John and his friends, the more we discovered that we needed to make even more progress. While we were trying to 'teach' our friends something about Our Lord and his love, using all the skill and special means at our disposal, we were forgetting that John had a voice himself, a voice that would speak, albeit in words sometimes difficult to comprehend. While we were 'giving' him ourselves, admittedly gladly and with great delight, we were stopping him giving us anything, except the rather passive affections and appreciation for which he became renowned.

This dawned on me with great force one day when a young autistic man called Sean did something that completely astounded us. He would say very little except, 'night, night', and it seemed impossible to communicate with him at all. He was playing with matches on the floor and was intently making them into words which were difficult to read because they were spelt out backwards and upside down. Once we deciphered his method, we discovered that he had clearly spelt out the words he must have seen on a signpost - 'Nottingham University'. On another occasion, a young lady called Francesca was hovering around a snooker table in our group leader's dining room. She was dying to have a go and we condescendingly allowed her. Eventually she potted a red ball, with great enthusiasm, and proceeded to name off the coloured balls in exact sequence.

The words of our own publication, '*Guidelines '77*' had come glaringly true in practice:
> *It is not a question of allowing handicapped persons to take part in the Church's life, but of seeking to learn from them, and from the unique gifts and talents which they alone contribute to the enriching of our lives.*

It was this realisation that formed the basis of the notion of 'contribution', and of the work with our friends becoming more outward-looking. Our limited expectations of John might have actually imprisoned him even further. To be glad in seeing him come to appreciate spiritual things and that life with God was a great thing, but what about his 'contribution', what could he give to us and others, and how could we enable him to do so? For many years John, and those in a similar situation to him, had become 'receivers' - people had given them time, treats, holidays and days out, with the result sometimes that they had come to expect this from their relationships with others, and not recognised their own responsibilities to give what is in them to others. It had never occurred to them, because no one had mentioned it before, but we should have done, we should have realised.

In March 1982, the Dublin Diocesan Education Council had published a very informative document which four years later came to be seen as more than a little prophetic.

> *Every parish has a number of people who are handicapped by some form of disability. Their presence in the Church and their contribution to society has been tolerated rather than appreciated. Their right to belong and to be different needs to be acknowledged. They do have a significant role in the upbuilding of the community, but this can only be realised if priests and parishioners use great ingenuity in enabling them to gain a sense of belonging by participating as recognised members of the parish at worship, and at all other events of parish life according to their capabilities... the need to fit into the local community as contributing members is deeply felt by persons who are handicapped and their families. The initiative to achieve this should come from the majority of parishioners... (Briefing, 1982).*

On the first weekend of Lent 1985, Cardinal Basil Hume accepted an invitation from our bishop to make an official visit to our diocese. The poor man's feet never touched the ground for three days, as he was whisked through five counties in a frenetic round of prayer and consultation. His visit culminated with a Mass for 3,000 young people in a large theatre in Leicester. The Loreto group was asked to take part, and we mimed the gospel of Jesus' temptation in the desert. The impact of this was stunning, and even the Cardinal was moved to speak a word of humble thanks.

It was at this moment, that it dawned on us that the liturgy was not simply to be celebrated with and for our friends, but also by them for others. They had become 'preachers of the Word' in a most dramatic and vivid way, using their own gifts and expressions to bring home the meaning of the Word of God to us in an entirely new manner. We are all called by God in baptism to make his name known to others, to receive and proclaim the Word, who is Jesus Christ. Here we could see people accepting this responsibility with devotion and enthusiasm. We had portrayed mimes of the scriptures on many occasions before, and on two occasions hour-long presentations of St. Matthew's Passion, but in this context, the effect had been more stunning than ever. It was done with conviction - of the heart and of the whole person. One woman said that she had, 'never heard the Word of God like this before.' The days of passive participation in the liturgy and life of the Church were gone for ever.

The year of 1986 marked a great turning point in John's personal life and in the work of our agency. John's parents had both died within 18 months of each other, with no provision made to look after him, save a promise to do so forced out of me by his mother on her death bed. Having to tell him of his beloved mother's death was a very taxing thing. He spent some time in a local hospital for mentally handicapped people, before the leader of our Loreto group and his wife took the bold step of borrowing a large sum of money, purchasing a house and setting up a residential community for twelve people, including their own daughter, Orla, after whom the community was named. This was the first such scheme operated as a private venture in this country and it has now become the model for countless others.

In one of the most moving moments of our long friendship, I shall never forget the first night when John settled down in his own bed and his own room. We prayed together for his parents, and he looked up to heaven when I mentioned their names. He held my hand as I said the words, '*John, this is your home now, for ever*,' and a tear of gratitude ran down his face. John's new family life has not been without difficulty, but it is full of happiness and loving care, for which we can all be grateful.

After this event, things began to move quickly. Three of our group joined a large number of young people in the production of a full-length play about the life and death of Fr. Jerzy Popieluszko. Some of it was featured on television. Ten years later, our friends are still able to speak the name of the priest and tell you about the play.

A project was conceived in Nottingham, and named after the great preacher, St. Paul, whereby our group would go into a parish on a given Sunday morning, and lead the prayer of the parish Sunday Mass, 'communicating' the Word of God and his message for that day in their own unique way. '*You did not choose me,*' said Jesus, '*No, I chose you, and I commissioned you to go out and bear fruit, fruit that will last*' - Our Lord's calling was not just to some people but to all people. That some did not accept it was their choice; others had not even been given the opportunity to accept the invitation until now. They did so gladly and joyfully, to great effect all around the city of Nottingham, and later in Derby as well. John was right at the heart of this; his speech is severely impaired, but his enthusiasm is infectious.

Time and time again we have come back to this notion of 'contribution' in our prayer and group meetings throughout the diocese. One example is the feast of Candlemas - '*Jesus calls us into this light; Jesus calls us to be his light for others*' - but how? By being peacemakers in our home, centre or community, through love and compassion, sensitivity to each other's needs and so on. Another is the time we met with our bishop and he commissioned over 300 people individually by name to, '*Share your gift; build the kingdom*' and they spent the next six months in groups discerning what precisely those gifts might be and how to use them.

The 'contribution' was not always a spiritual one. There were other ways in which this notion could be reflected. In 1990, the group in Nottingham was asked to raise some money for a Franciscan nun working in a children's clinic in Nairobi. They did so by presenting a '40's evening', the centrepiece of which was a specially scripted version of the TV programme, 'Allo! Allo!' This provided the ideal vehicle for people with learning and speech difficulties, as many of the parts have repeated one-line speeches. One young man spent the fortnight before, each day in his training centre hiding under tables, emerging, lifting his spectacles and saying, *'It is I, Leclerc!'* Costumes were borrowed from Central TV and the play was presented in two centres, Nottingham and Derby. Even now, six years later, one young man, who played the policeman, Crabtree, remembers all his lines, word for word, and will gladly reel them off at the slightest invitation! Another young man got up on the stage after the play and made a spontaneous speech of thanks to the producers!

A production of 'Scrooge' in 1993 enabled our Derby group to make its 'contribution' to the local community in a way in which they all enjoyed. Many people with speech impairments struggled bravely to speak their lines, and they loved the dressing up, the lights and the make-up. The audiences were thrilled.

To mark the Decade of Evangelisation, the agency decided to begin and foster a 'Partnership Project' with CAFOD, to help the starving people of Ethiopia. A year-long programme of education took place, in which we learned about the Ethiopian people and their way of life, their suffering and their hopes for the future. An Ethiopian Christmas dinner was a particularly inventive way of bringing this home to all of us. We also had CAFOD boxes on hand for each club night, so that we could 'contribute' the fruits of our self-denial to Ethiopia, through CAFOD.

On several occasions, our groups have taken part in the Trent Walk, an overnight sponsored walk in aid of 18 local charities working with disabled people, which the agency organises and which has raised £200,000 since it began 15 years ago. John has great difficulty in walking, but he has bravely, if very slowly, completed his distance of seven and a half miles and was very proud of himself when he got to the finish. We also spent a lot of time together publicising the event and working in local supermarkets to bring it to the attention of the general public. Tin-rattling is one of John's special enjoyments!

Each year for the past 8 years the Nottingham group has hosted its own Bank Holiday Monday Fun Day - an inexpensive day out for up to 10,000 local people. John and his friends are heavily involved in running stalls and taking responsibility for different activities during the day. He has made a great impression on the visitors, and you can see them obviously thinking twice when they realise that people like John actually do want to be 'givers' as well as 'receivers', and that they are not content to just sit in a corner and let it happen around them.

Our latest 'contribution' project has been a most moving and innovative one. Every year, a Faith & Light Day takes place all over the world on the nearest Sunday to the feast of Candlemas. The liturgy tends to be the same, and we have virtually exhausted ways of celebrating it with our friends. Last year, we were inspired to celebrate the 'Dance of the Light', to express in music and movement the light of God moving over the face of the earth, and the ways in which we can be brought into it ourselves, and thence share it with others. A beautiful dance to the music of the West End show, 'Riverdance', was presented, and the whole Mass took place to music. It was a truly inspiring experience which none of those present will ever forget.

Looking ahead, we need now to think carefully about how we may proceed with our friends in the service of Our Lord and each other, and about what may prevent us from developing our philosophy of 'contribution' with them. There are many factors to take into consideration including community, responsibility, faith and acceptance.

A Sense of Community

We may argue that in general, a sense of 'community' has now all but disappeared from our society. People are finding themselves more isolated from each other, hardly ever seeing their family or neighbours. The ever more competitive work environment has the drawback of making us more single-minded, to the extent that we fail to recognise each other's needs and how we might respond to them. For our special friends there are added difficulties. Many people with a handicapping condition are forced to concentrate their attention on themselves and on the management of that condition. Many with learning difficulties have been living at home, where they are the centre of the family, which can make them very selfish and self-centred and thus uncaring about those around them. Community life may not be so easy for them either.

A Sense of Responsibility

This follows from our view on community. For years, we have fought for John and his friends to be able to be treated as persons, with all the rights and choices that are involved in this, but we may forget that where there are rights, there are also responsibilities. Without responsible behaviour, we cannot exist as a society, law and order breaks down, and hurt can easily be caused. We cannot talk of our friends as 'contributors' unless they are brought to recognise their responsibilities to each other, and thus to see the importance and necessity of what they have to give. The fact that John and many of his friends now live in communities of one sort or another should help to make them alive to their responsibilities to each other, and maybe this is where a concentration on the whole matter of reconciliation - personally and sacramentally may come to bear fruit.

A Sense of Faith

This may not always be present. Many of our friends have been brought up in a non-Church background. Faith has not been part of their family lifestyle, and therefore it may take years to develop both moral attitudes and a living relationship with Our Lord. We need to accept this situation and not presume anything. Many people like John, however, do have a spiritual background, they do appreciate the presence of Our Lord in their lives, and they are keen to respond to His promptings. If people come to join our groups, they do so with full knowledge of what we are about: we are not just an opportunity for social gathering; we seek to be living communities based on the gospel and the way of the Lord. There is no need ever to make an apology for this, only to work on what is there already in the minds and hearts of our special friends and their families.

A Sense of Acceptance

You can only give of yourself to people who wish to receive from you, and the most important factor in the future is whether society will wish our friends to 'contribute' to its life or not. We have to say that already some of the signs are alarming, and that there is a distinct possibility of our returning to the situation with which we started, nearly 25 years ago. In a climate where the accent is very much on what you can get for yourself, the weak will be marginalised once more, and those who cannot compete will be relegated to the fringes. Job losses for able-bodied people mean less opportunity for those with lesser cognitive and physical abilities. When speed is all that counts, those who go more slowly may be rejected. When performance is the essential work ethic, those who do not perform with so much ambition, drive, even ruthlessness, may have no place. It is all very well in these politically correct days of adjusting our language so that our friends with disabilities (now called 'differently abled'!) are not offended, but what if this is at the expense of less opportunities for them in housing, employment and 'contribution'?

Much of what is done is dishonest. Integration of people with special difficulties into mainstream education is very laudable in theory, but not if the main reason is a financial, cost-cutting one. This must be done with great care and patience, and funds should be made available to adapt buildings, provide necessary therapeutic facilities and the staff required to offer the right sort of care. Sadly, this is not happening yet. The economic climate is leading to proposals to close adult training centres and day centres. The result of this is that our friends will have nowhere to go and no chance to learn and improve themselves. The 'Care in the Community' model is highly suspect. Many of John's friends do have the chance to live in small group homes or even on their own with support, but often the support is provided 'on the cheap' by unqualified people in insufficient numbers. Our cities have become increasingly more full of people wandering around looking lost and forlorn. Is this care in the community?

The most sinister 'solution' to this economic problem has already begun to take horrifying shape. Many people with handicapping conditions are simply not being allowed to be born. Their 'problems' have been detected in the womb before birth, and their parents are being persuaded that they will have no 'real quality of life', so what is euphemistically called a 'termination' is the only real alternative. Better luck next time. This sad and sorry state of affairs has now reached epidemic proportions with the result that the birth rate for children with particular forms of handicap, like Down Syndrome, has dropped almost to nil. There will still be, however low we sink in our respect for the unborn, people with conditions that are caused during birth, just afterwards, or through rare illness or traumatic accident, so there will always be people with disabilities, even if we feel as a society that we can no longer 'afford' to treat them as human beings. There will always be people like John, and thank God for him. But where the 'quality of life' for John and those like him is determined by the attitude of others, by respect for the person as a person with his own life to lead, his own choices to make, and his 'contribution' to give, lack of resources can never be used as an excuse for not accepting a responsibility which is the duty of all of us as human beings: to treat everyone equally.

'A man came... sent by God' - I firmly believe that Almighty God has sent us John to teach us something about Him and about ourselves. '...He was not the light, only a witness to speak for the light...' - he is sent to show us what is really important and how it might be achieved. That precisely is his 'contribution'. To build a better world for our future is not the task of politicians or accountants. It is a responsibility that lies in the heart of every human being, every individual person. We all need to look into our hearts and see what is there: perhaps they have become empty and void, saturated with the consumerism that has now run its course and failed to bring the peace and happiness it promised. All around us there are people like John who cannot compete, who do not realise the value of achievement and status, of wealth and prestige, who have no need of the things that the rest of us seem to think are so necessary for living. They have more to teach us than anyone.

They live their lives simply, and show us where we have been wrong, where our values have been misplaced, where the soul of society has been lost, and our whole sense of direction misguided. These people are not 'mistakes'; they are here for a purpose - to show us how to make and live in a kinder world. There is a kinder world, but it starts in the heart of each of us, in our willingness to give, to listen, to sacrifice, to love, to eliminate all in us that would subdue, dominate or marginalise others, all that makes us think that we are better than them, and that they are of no worth. It is a world where the poor teach the rich, the hungry feed the replete, and the homeless challenge the housed.

The 'witness' for the Light would speak to us, show us the way, 'contribute' to our lives and the true richness we need, if only we will let him speak, and listen to him.

REFERENCES

Battye, L. (1976). The Chatterley Syndrome, in *The Handicapped Person in the Community*. London: The Open University.
Briefing (1982). Published by The Catholic Media Office.
Nolan, C. (1987). *Under The Eye of The Clock*. London: Weidenfield and Nicholson.

Biographical Note

Father Frank Daly has been working with people with special needs since March 1972. He is the founder and Director of the Nottingham Diocesan Services for Special Needs (1976), the parish priest of the Community of Our Lady of Lourdes, Mickleover, Derby, the Director of the Catholic Chaplaincy Team to the Southern Derbyshire Mental Health Unit, and the Dean of the Derby Deanery.

3 PONDERING THE ANOMALY OF GOD'S LOVE — ETHICAL REFLECTIONS ON ACCESS TO THE SACRAMENTS

Paul J. Wadell, C.P.

A Christmas Story

"A child is born to us, a son is given us", but it was not the son they expected. Two months early and gasping for life, this Christmas morning gift took them by surprise and turned their lives inside out. His manger was a small, flat table in the neonatal unit where children are not expected to survive. He was not wrapped in swaddling clothes but in needles, tape and tubes that covered every inch of his innocent flesh. One look at him brought one to reverence and softened one's heart. Stalked by death and wounded by a life that began too soon, to behold him was to encounter holiness, to come before the presence of God and be awed. As the shepherds and the wise gathered around the Christ child to ponder the mystery of God's great love, this was Christ's child too. In this tiny gift, utterly helpless and shockingly needy, humanity and God came together again. God was lying there, fighting for life, pleading for the world's recognition; it was an incarnation, another Christmas morning.

The child's name is Carl. He was born with cerebral palsy and he is my nephew. But on that Christmas morning he was also a sacrament, God speaking to us in cryptic, saving ways. Hidden in an affliction that would mark him for life was a word worth hearing, a grace ready to redeem. Like every sacrament, this outward sign of rebellious muscles and determined heart bore a secret gospel. God was in this fragile flower, beckoning to us with some astonishing news about things human and divine. In this Christmas morning gift, transparent with neediness too flagrant to be denied, was a surprising, liberating gospel about God and ourselves. Here was not one of the strong, but a child of sacred incompleteness. Here was a beloved of God with frailty and fracture that could not be disguised. Here was God where we least expected; hidden away in the lowly, shrouded in the harmless who disturb. It is through such misbegotten that God speaks to us the most.

The eloquence of God is often embodied in those whom we tend to dismiss. We think of persons with developmental disabilities as anomalies. If they are sacraments,[1] however, manifestations of God and manifestations of ourselves, perhaps the real deviants are those who fail to heed the message they convey. This is a book about access to the sacraments for persons in the Church with disabilities, but in order to understand how to address that question we need to turn things around. What if those with developmental disabilities are sacraments of God's life and it is we, the allegedly able-bodied, who must first have access to them? We will never understand our obligations in justice to persons with disabilities unless we scrutinise what they reveal about God and ourselves.

We begin with heads turned and hearts opened. Our focus in assessing who should have access to God in the sacraments is not on the people we take to be normal, but on the needy ones in our midst who stray from the norm just as much as our God does. To understand rightly what access to the sacraments mean, we must begin with those who mirror best both God and ourselves. Disabled persons reflect back to us a different understanding of ourselves and a different understanding of God. In pondering that reflection we learn why access to the sacraments in the Church is something determined by God, not ourselves. In this chapter, we shall examine this question of sacramental access for persons with disabilities by asking (1) what do people with physical and mental disabilities teach us about ourselves? (2) what do they teach us about God and what God wants for us? and (3) what do they teach us about what it means to be the church?

Befriending the Ones We Usually Exclude

We must begin not by discussing but by befriending. In order to understand the moral dimensions of access to the sacraments for persons in the Church with developmental disabilities, the critical first step is to befriend the ones we normally exclude, or perhaps better, to allow them to befriend us. In Christopher Nolan's poignant and beautiful autobiographical novel *Under the Eye of the Clock*, Joseph Meehan, born mute and crippled, writes of Alex Clark, "who belonged to that great able-bodied world" (Nolan, 1987, 4), and who "devoted time and trouble to not only pushing Joseph's wheelchair, but to being one of Joseph's acute and early friends." Meehan remembers how "Alex brought his strength into play and sacking Joseph's cross of much of its sting... helped his friend to sample some of the good things of life" (Nolan, 1987, 5). Through Alex "he captured again the security left when a mute crippled boy has a brave vocal friend" (Nolan, 1987, 6).

But what happens to the able-bodied when they receive the offer of friendship that comes from the mute and the crippled? If Joseph Meehan was able to share in the world of the able-bodied through the kindness of Alex Clark, then it is through friendship with the Joseph Meehan's of this world that we enter the world of those we seldom take time to understand. If we are not to be handicapped by our fear of those who initially seem so different, we have to cross a boundary and risk entering their world. Being befriended by persons with disabilities is like entering another country. It is foreign terrain; its landscape looks so different. We are confronted by alien customs. We meet people with a novel understanding of what it means to be. It is unsettling, but we must be willing to listen to them and learn from them. Being open to the friendship of those we normally avoid is essential for discovering what God wants for all of us and what it means to treat such people justly.

Persons with disabilities force us to think of ourselves differently. Entering their world, our self is reflected back to us in ways we normally do not glimpse or work hard to obscure. More than anything, they show us that we are persons of individuality and strength, not when we are autonomous and self-sufficient, but, in M. Scott Peck's marvellous phrase, when we learn "the power of helplessness" (Peck, 1990, 77). As Stephen Solaris, the brain-damaged, bedridden prophet of Peck's novel *A Bed by the Window* reminds us, those who are powerful are those who have "come to terms with their helplessness (Peck, 1990, 78).

The idea that the powerful and the strong are those who have embraced their helplessness offers us a different understanding of what it means to be a person. It may also be the most significant gift the disabled bring us. Human beings are those who have come to grips with their need, not ashamed to confess their indigence and no longer embarrassed by inabilities. This is the first lesson about personhood we learn when we enter the world of those people we normally fear. We cannot be persons unless we know our helplessness and acknowledge our need. Anything else is a dangerous deception. Once we accept the power of our helplessness we begin to understand why persons with disabilities are a metaphor for all of us; indeed, we realise that if we see them as an anomaly it is only because we profoundly misunderstand ourselves.

Sometimes we want to misunderstand because we fear what the truth reveals. Perhaps we exclude the disabled and refuse to grant them access to our lives and our communities because we do not want to accept what they tell us about ourselves. Their disabilities frighten us not because we do not know how to help them belong, but because being with them discloses how false and misguided is the dominant understanding of ourselves. And so we work to construct a world that vetoes their presence and overrules their pleas to belong. We do this under the pretext of protecting them from harm, but the truth may be that we want to protect ourselves from what they have to teach us. In *Under the Eye of the Clock*, Joseph Meehan reflects on this strategy of exclusion when he learns his application for school has once again been rejected:

> *Someone always vetoes his application thought Joseph... someone always vetoes; someone normal; someone beautiful; someone blessed by normality; someone administering the rusty mind's rules of yesteryear;... someone Christian worst of all, boasted ascetic, one of the head-strokers poor child, God love him. Ah! God is good, never shuts one door but he opens another;... someone versed in the art of saying no;... someone able to say no to a dumb cripple; someone always says no (Nolan, 1987, 12-13).*

Unmasking a Heretical View of the Self

The last thing we want is to learn the power of our helplessness. Our culture promotes an anthropology that says to be human is to be "free from all unanswered needs" (McGill, 1987, 14). We rebel against limitations, refuse to be deflected by the unexpected, and insist that any incompleteness can be overcome. Our normative view of the self suggests an ideology of the strong. More often than not, we believe we can be fulfilled in all our capacities, constantly growing and never diminishing, lacking nothing and in masterful control of our lives. In the ideology of the strong, frailty is not accepted as part of the human condition, nor is misfortune or tragedy; such unhappiness comes only to those who plan poorly or choose wrongly. There is no room for failure in the ideology of the strong; indeed, "a person must try to prove by his or her own existence that failure does not belong essentially to life" (McGill, 1987, 18).

This is the understanding of self dominating Western culture, and it helps us understand why the unhidden frailty of the disabled is such an affront. In the ideology of the strong, the "normal" person shows no sign of debility and acknowledges no helplessness. Arthur McGill calls such persons the "bronze people" (McGill, 1987, 26). In the ideology of the strong, they are paradigms of human flourishing. The bronze people are never deflected by chance or ravaged by misfortune; indeed, they betray not the slightest hint of incompletion. With them "all traces of weakness, debility, ugliness, and helplessness must be kept away from every part of a person's life" (McGill, 1987, 26). Disabled by nothing, they live by their own power and include others by choice but never by need. As Stanley Hauerwas reflects: "We seek to be strong. We seek to be self-possessed. We seek to deny that we depend on others for our existence. We will be self-reliant and we resent and avoid those who do not seek to be like us - the strong" (Hauerwas, 1986, 175).

This vision of personhood which dominates our culture illuminates why anyone less than perfectly whole is a scandal. The most obvious truth about persons with mental or physical disabilities is that they are not creatures of total self-possession, but persons who clearly depend on others. They live from their

---

neediness; everything about them communicates their dependence on people who care and are willing to live. But bronze people depend on no one. Their identity comes not from the relationships they have with others, but from their self-sufficiency. They could never understand Joseph Meehan's whispered prayer, "Do with me what you can... I can be but my feeble self" (Nolan, 1987, 25), because they could never countenance such an unabashed confession of need.

We exclude persons with disabilities from our midst because they unmask the pretensions with which we live. We label them as disabled or retarded or deviant not because they are less than human, but because to accept them would be to learn that our sense of normalcy must be radically revised. They show us how little we know about what it means to be human and challenge us to turn from ignorance by learning from them. We need access to them much more than they to us, because in our self-deception we hardly realise how disabling the ideology of the strong really is.

Perhaps the greatest injustice inflicted on persons with disabilities is to exclude them not for their sake but for ours. We keep them at a distance because we do not want to see that we too are helpless and needy; our lives too are fragile, vulnerable, and assailable by chance. Because those with disabilities expose our definitions of normalcy as pathetically misguided, we label them in a way that justifies their exclusion. We call them disabled not because they are helpless, but because they are so glaringly other than what we think a normal person should be. What they refuse to hide scares us. We fail to grant them access to our lives - and sometimes even to God - because we are profoundly uncomfortable with the realities they symbolise. They offend us because they are willing to be what we fear.

Even worse, they do not try to hide their needs. They are not self-sufficient, they are not self-possessed, they are in need. Even more, they do not evidence the proper shame for being so. They simply assume that they are what they are and they need to provide no justification for being such. It is almost as if they have been given a natural grace to be free from the regret most of us feel for our neediness (Hauerwas 1986, 176).

Human Life Is a Resting-in-Neediness

Persons with disabilities bring a different sense of what is normal. Their lives testify that the most inescapable fact about being human is to be in need. This does not mean that the disabled are initially more accepting of their neediness than anyone else, for indeed they can resist it as well as the rest of us; however, their lives show us that being in need is not a disability, but a fundamental fact of being human which all of us are ultimately unable - and should have no desire - to hide.[2] Arthur McGill poignantly summarises this perspective by suggesting that "human life is a resting-in-neediness" (McGill, 1987, 83). No one teaches this better than those in our midst with needs too glaring to suppress. As Dianne Bergant suggests in 'Come, let us go up to the mountain of the Lord' p13-32, from *Developmental Disability and Sacramental Access - New Paradigms for Sacramental Encounters* persons with disabilities do not see neediness as something to escape but as the starting point for understanding rightly who we are. We begin to know ourselves when we acknowledge our indigence, when we confess the incompleteness at the core of our being.

Unlike the bronze people, persons with disabilities espouse an anthropology which says each of us is inescapably incomplete and unavoidably dependent on others for our existence.

Bianca has a Mind of her Own

Bianca was nine when she first came for catechesis. She was disruptive and violent. She would kick and yell and try to climb on the altar when the community gathered to worship. Bianca was contrary and stubborn. Because of her lack of verbal communication and her stubbornness and because the group she joined had been together for two years, Bianca was quickly isolated. She was withdrawn from the group.

After two years, Bianca's parents asked again if she could join a group for catechesis. She was able to join a group with the ongoing support of someone that she trusted and who was also trusted by the group. During the next three years Bianca came to enjoy the games, drawing, music and rhythm of the group experience. For her, catechesis became synonymous with the friendship she had experienced.

At the beginning when the group assembled, Bianca would go into a corner and turn her back on everyone. She would hide when the group ate or would eat after the group left. But she loved the activities of the group, the slides and pictures that helped her understand that "Jesus is with us." She had made such good progress that her parents suggested that she be prepared for first Communion with her special friend Freddy.

The group took six months to prepare the Eucharistic celebration. They created all the symbols, giving attention to preparing the table. Invitations were addressed to all the friends who had shared in other festivities of the group. Freddy was particularly happy inviting everyone and talking about his celebration. Bianca seemed to share his joy.

Everything was ready for the Eucharistic celebration. But not Bianca. She refused to eat even though it was clear that she understood in some way that the Eucharist was more than eating food. There was no fuss. Bianca just said no. Her parents were shocked and discouraged. So were the catechists. Even when they held a quiet liturgy for the small group she had grown to trust, she still refused. Bianca spoke affectionately to the adults present; she was obviously happy to be part of the group but she would not open her mouth for the bread.

Unlike those who find their identity in self-possession, the disabled choose to find life in relationships because they know that it is only in being open to others and receiving from them that we can live. From the perspective of the Joseph Meehans of the world, neediness is intrinsic to our nature. Thus the anomaly resides not with the needy, but with those deathly afraid of saying "I am incomplete."

To be able to rest in our neediness and find power in our helplessness is key to becoming whole. We do not secure any healthy sense of what it is to be human through the arrogance of self-sufficiency, but through the honesty which confesses that to be is to need. Such a perspective turns everything around, making the people we wish to exclude "normal" and everyone offended by their openness "strange." Persons with disabilities are gifts in our midst because they teach us how we should live if we are to discover the grace of being human. Befriending them may bring a crisis of identity for us, but it is a redemptive crisis.

Jesus: Living Through the Power of God

Jesus, as exemplar of humanity and primary sacrament, was willing to acknowledge his absolute dependence on God. If Jesus was perfectly human because his whole life represented best how we should live, integral to his perfection was the ability to rest in his neediness and find power in his incompleteness. It was, in fact, knowledge of this necessity that accounted for his extraordinary openness to God. Jesus lived not in himself, but by virtue of the life he constantly received from God. McGill calls this his "ecstatic identity" (McGill, 1987, 70): at every moment of his life Jesus lived not from his own power but from the power of God. What made Jesus unique was his ability to acknowledge his need, and that, in turn, opened him to the fullness of life God wants for all of us. Jesus lived "not by virtue of anything that [was] his own," but "by virtue of what the Father continually communicate[d] to him" (McGill, 1987, 70). Jesus had power by resting in his neediness; it was the opening through which God entered his life and was the secret of his perfection.

What made Jesus unique was that he never saw life as his own possession or his existence as self-achievement; rather, as McGill writes, he knew "the constituting activity of God as the constant and ongoing condition of his own being. Jesus never [had] his own being; [was] continually receiving it. ... He [was] only as one who [kept] receiving himself from God" (McGill, 1987, 50). Jesus challenged our normal sense of existence. He showed us that we have life the same way he did: not by ourselves but through the agency of God. Our identity can be ecstatic too when we live not in virtue of ourselves but only in virtue of the life we are willing to receive. Like Jesus, we can live through the constant communication of God's love. As McGill says, "My 'I am' necessarily and constantly includes God's activity of constituting me" (McGill, 1987, 51).

Seeing Jesus as the norm of all things human reverses our sense of being human. Our neediness is not something about which to be ashamed, but the door through which God's love enters our lives. Our dependence is not a weakness, but a prerequisite for fullness of life; indeed, the truth of our nature is our absolute need to receive. To the extent we are able to acknowledge our need, we receive the life which blesses us far more than we ever could ourselves. To be ashamed of our need is thus to be needlessly deprived.

Is this not, for example, the meaning of the Eucharist? The Eucharist invites us into the life-giving love of God. As a community of faith, we gather in Eucharist not because we are able-bodied and self-sufficient, but precisely because we are flawed, indigent, and frail people who hunger for the bread of life God so richly provides.

Furthermore, the Eucharist testifies that if the most basic fact of our existence is our radical indigence, it is equally true that God's response to our neediness is never-ending, life-giving love. This is the "new identity" of which the gospels speak: finding life not in self-possession, resistance, anxiety, or hardness of heart, but in gratitude for the love God longs to give. To move from anxiety and fear to openness and trust is to suffer the change of heart necessary to share God's life. "The love that passes understanding is available to us in the very act of our being, because we are constantly receiving that from our God" (McGill, 1987, 52), but only those able to rest in their neediness know this.

We need persons with physical and intellectual disabilities in our midst, and certainly in our worship, in order to remember who we are. In their willingness to confess their dependence on others - and indeed their dependence on God - they are sacraments for us: outward signs of a more genuine humanity. God speaks to us through them, calling our attention to a more truthful way of being. We find deep truths about ourselves in unexpected places. Perhaps the most important truth disabled persons teach us, is that from our neediness we receive abundant life. We need them at our side when we worship, not out of kindness to them, but as a graced reminder of why we die without the bread of life. In befriending them we embrace the truth about ourselves to which redemption responds: there is a need in us only God's love can fulfil.

The Great Undertaking of the God with a Tender Heart

In Under the Eye of the Clock, Joseph Meehan comments that "great undertakings require great tender rescuers with great tender hearts" (Nolan, 1987, 23). He is talking about going to school with the able-bodied, and the "tender rescuers with great tender hearts" are the teachers and students who befriend him. But this is also a way of understanding what God does for us in Christ. Here the great undertaking is the redemption of the world and the tender rescuer with the tender heart is God whose tenderness comes to us through Christ, the Spirit, the sacraments, and the goodness of others.

Ethical reflections on the sacraments should not begin with explanations of what they mean or who should receive them, but with a recognition of what God does for us in Christ. In other words, we do not define the sacraments, God does. It is only by first pondering what God undertakes and accomplishes through Christ, the primary sacrament, that we rightly know what the other sacraments mean and how we are to respond to them. God's saving activity in Christ defines the substance of the sacraments; therefore, questions about who should receive them are answered not through our own sense of appropriateness but by discerning the overriding intention of God. The question is not whom do we invite to fellowship with Christ, but who is God seeking and what is God striving to achieve.

The sacraments, as manifestations of the saving presence of Christ, seek the full liberation of God in every aspect of our lives. As Mark R. Francis (1994), Celebrating the Sacrament with those with Developmental Disability p73–93 in Developmental Disabilities and Sacramental Access - New Paradigms for Sacramental Encounters, observes, each sacrament provides the possibility of bringing God wholly to life in us by uniting us with the life, death, and resurrection of Christ. As mediations of the paschal mystery, the sacraments work for the full flowering of God's redemptive life in our hearts and in our world. It is through them that the great undertaking of redemption takes place. Thus, as Mary Therese Harrington suggests in this book (chapter 5) the core of the sacraments is not our sense of what we need, but God's relentless desire to offer us friendship and life. From this perspective, no one in the Church should be denied access to God's gift of salvation.

It is especially in Jesus that we understand the great undertaking of the God of tender heart. God comes to us in Christ to offer us not just a better life, but God's own life. Through the incarnation our life is not enhanced, it is transfigured, for in this offer of friendship with Christ we are invited to enter the life of God. In Christ and the Spirit we are made new creations. To transform us through love is God's mission in the world, and through the sacraments God continues the divine ministry of freeing us from death and filling us with life. The sacraments exist for the same reason that the incarnation occurred: God desires access to our hearts and to our world. Each of the sacraments testifies that we matter to God, and that God will not rest until each one of us has access to the love that saves.

In justice we are owed access to God because God desires to be accessible to us. The sacraments articulate how much God wants to be part of our lives. God wants not only to give us life, God wants to know us in the special friendship of charity, working on our behalf, seeking our good, being completely devoted to what is best for us. Christ, the primary sacrament, and all the other sacraments testify to this. They eloquently depict the personal, passionate love God has for each of us. They capture the extremes to which God goes to be part of our lives. The gospel fact is that God loves everybody. People who love us want to be with us, and it is no different for God. The heart of God's saving ministry in Christ and the Spirit is to seek communion with humanity. This is God's abiding intention revealed in Christ and it is to this that the life and energy of God are primarily devoted. God is forever at work to establish friendship and communion with us and among us. That God lives to love us is manifest in the sacraments; and the principal duty of the Church is to facilitate, not frustrate, God's intention.

Redemption: An Act of Love, A Gift of Absolute Need

To appreciate the great undertaking of God we must remember our need for redemption. The "great tender rescuer" is God and God's act of rescuing continues through the sacraments. God reaches out to us because we need to be saved. From God's side it is an act of love, but from our side it is a gift which we absolutely need. As much as God wants to share in our life, we die if we do not share in God's. We stand in need of a rescue because we cannot ransom ourselves. As Dietrich Bonhoeffer reminds us, in ourselves we are destitute and dead. "Help must come from the outside, and it has come and comes daily and anew in the Work of Jesus Christ, bringing redemption, righteousness, innocence, and blessedness" (Bonhoeffer 1954, 22).

One of the reasons persons with disabilities may make us uncomfortable is that they remind us that we are stricken too. Living after the Fall, all of us are misbegotten creatures who "flew into the incorrect night" (DeRosa, 1980, 8). We share a common affliction: wayward and misguided, wounded by the contradictions lodged in our hearts. It is our kinship in sin that makes us needy, our solidarity in corruption that leaves us begging for a rescue we can only receive. The earth is a place for the fallen and a home for the flawed. Its citizens are all those disabled by weakness and incompletion, debilitated by a disease of the spirit Christians call sin. We carry the marks of the infirm, walking about in weakness and need too glaring to be concealed. We feel currents of disorder in our hearts, forces of corruption which leaves us ensnared in behaviour that brings more sadness than joy. As sacraments of neediness, persons with disabilities remind us that all of us are flawed and imperfect, needing to be rescued, healed, and brought to perfect life by perfect love.

Gathered about the altar we are a communion of sinners more than saints. Looking about, we glimpse our fellowship with the fallen. Here all people are one. Here all pretence of righteousness is stripped away as we who have been initiated into our own frailty extend our hands to the God who saves. At the moment we see ourselves as we are, none of us healthy, none of us whole. Our eyes are opened to the disability all share. Through sin we have been lured off centre and need to be restored. Sin constitutes a disordering of all dimensions of our nature, leaving us infirm and feeble, needing to be fortified by grace. If Joseph Meehan suffered with rebellious muscles, all of us suffer with rebellious hearts. We need to be calmed, blessed, shriven, and redeemed.

The Sacraments: Lifelines to God's Love

The sacraments, as expressions of God's great undertaking in Christ, are acts of rescue and manifestations of God's relentless desire to have access to our lives. It is through the sacraments that God reaches us in our need and delivers us from our exile. Stranded in sin and needing deliverance, we wait in hope for some lifeline to God's love. As symbols of our sharing in the paschal mystery, the sacraments are lifelines to the love that saves.

Questions about accessibility to the sacraments have no meaning unless we remember the priority of God's desire to be accessible to us in baptism, forgiveness, and bread and wine. The startling and crucial point in questions of sacramental access is not that we can approach God, but rather that God humbly approaches us. Though the aim of the sacraments is to rescue us by making us new, the first transfiguration belongs to God; indeed, in the Eucharist the God of the universe rests in the hands of sinners. As Joseph Meehan reflects after receiving Communion, "Communion too brought his comforter within his grasp... Communion served grand purpose, serving to bring God to him and him to serve God" (Nolan, 1987, 59).

Our comforter is always within our grasp. Each of the sacraments serves the grand purpose of bringing our rescuer within reach. They underscore the shocking vulnerability of God. Ours is not a God tucked safely away in the heavens, unmolested by the terrors of life, but a God who surrenders so completely to our needs as to be held in our hands and fed to our hearts. The vulnerability of God is so extreme that through the sacraments we can take advantage of God, which is precisely what God wants. God is utterly accessible in bread and wine and every other sacramental symbol because God wants us to take advantage of the love that redeems. What is almost blasphemous about the sacraments is that they make God so easy to approach. Through them God is exposed and handed over. Collectively, the image of God communicated through the sacraments is that of a love of endless ingenuity that will do whatever is necessary to be with us. The sacraments remind us that the omnipresence of God is the incarnate accessibility of God.

The Eucharist is the point of God's greatest vulnerability, the sacrament in which God is delivered into hands that can caress or crush. But it is exactly this absolute accessibility of God which demonstrates how much God wants us to take to heart a love that saves. Scobie, a character in Graham Greene's novel *The Heart of the Matter*, captures this insight:

> *It seemed to him for a moment cruelly unfair of God to have exposed himself in this way, a man, a wafer of bread, first in the Palestinian villages and now here in the hot port, there, everywhere, allowing man to have his will of Him. Christ had told the rich young man to sell all and follow Him, but that was an easy rational step compared with this that God had taken, to put Himself at the mercy of men who hardly knew the meaning of the word. How desperately God must love, he thought with shame (Greene, 1971, 213).*

The unflinching accessibility God expressed in such tenderness and vulnerability may also mean that God - like all of us who are God's images - is not an utterly independent being who remains unmoved and unchanging, but a God of supreme relationality who not only finds life in loving us, but is also changed by that love. This is another reason persons with disabilities are sacraments for us. In them we see God, not because they are necessarily holy, but because like them God is not afraid to confess neediness, dependence, and a great desire to be loved. To be with them is to acquire access to God, because they communicate so beautifully that God does not claim self-sufficiency and is not ashamed to acknowledge the desire and need to be loved. They witness a facet of God we often forget: God's love saves us, but our love gives God life.

> *Quite simply, the challenge of learning to know, to be with, and care for the retarded is nothing less than learning to know, be with, and love God. God's face is the face of the retarded; God's body is the body of the retarded; God's being is that of the retarded. For the God we Christians must learn to worship is not a god of self-sufficient power,*

a god who in self-possession needs no one; rather ours is a God who needs a people, who needs a son. Absoluteness of being or power is not a work of the God we have come to know through the cross of Christ (Hauerwas 1986, 178).

The Church as Sacrament: A Community Gathered in Christ

There is a scene in Under the Eye of the Clock in which Joseph Meehan, in a moment of great discouragement and fear, looks to the cross and says, "God, would you be afraid if you were me?" (Nolan, 1987, 49). The answer to Joseph's question may depend on the kind of community Christians are willing to be. We have suggested throughout this chapter that God would not fear entering the crippled body of Joseph Meehan because God already has. If the Joseph Meehans of the world are sacraments of God's presence, God is always there with them, but perhaps they need the love and acceptance of other Christians to know this.

If such is the case, who should we be for one another? Standing together, the most obvious truth about us is not that some are disabled and others are not, but that we share a kinship in need and a kinship in Christ. Our identity comes not through the strength of our muscles or the sharpness of our minds, but in Christ who brings us together. The Church is a community of those gathered not by choice but by grace. We are there only because God has summoned us in Christ. As John Huels, OSM (1994) Canonical Rights to the Sacraments p94–115, says, all of us, whether strong or feeble, healthy or weak, ought to enjoy absolute equality in this community of faith because each of us has entered through the summoning grace of Christ.

If we are a community formed from a common calling, this means we belong to one another and are accountable to one another. We have been given one another by Christ to witness the love and justice of Christ and be faithful to the ways of Christ. God has entrusted all of us to each other, and thus we owe one another nothing less than the love and forgiveness God has given us. But the crucial fact is that God's choice of us precedes and must govern our choice of one another. It is God acting through Christ who constitutes the community of faith, and it is God's actions which must shape and determine our own; in short, whoever is acceptable to God must certainly be acceptable to us. As Bonhoeffer observes, "We have one another only through Christ, but through Christ we do have one another, wholly, and for all eternity" (Bonhoeffer, 1954, 26). If this is true, certain things follow. If God's action determines membership in the Church, denying persons with physical or mental disabilities access to this community and its sacraments contravenes what God desires. This is behind Bonhoeffer's comment that "every Christian community must realize that not only do the weak need the strong, but also that the strong cannot exist without the weak. The elimination of the weak is the death of fellowship" (Bonhoeffer, 1954, 94).

The strong cannot exist without the weak, nor the weak without the strong, because in a fellowship constituted, not by human selectiveness but by the graciousness of God, every person is indispensable. The strength and vitality of the community is not in its members, but in the love that has gathered them. To exclude anyone is to act against the strategies of divine love by making our whim more important than God's will. With the Church it is all or nothing. Either we accept all those God chooses to belong or we come something other than God's Church. Either we are the community of all those ransomed by Christ, or we are a community of our own choosing: a fraternal organisation perhaps, but hardly the people of God. "In a Christian community everything depends upon whether each individual is an indispensable link in a chain. Only when even the smallest link is securely interlocked is the chain unbreakable" (Bonhoeffer, 1954, 94).

The Church is faithful to the love of God when it realises everyone is indispensable to God, and thus should be indispensable to us. We must train ourselves to behold one another as God does. Is this how we see one another? Is this how we behold persons with disabilities? In order to see anyone as God sees them, we must free ourselves of the idolatry which holds that anyone lovely must be just like us. Our tendency is to deem acceptable whoever is fashioned in our image instead of the image of God. We use our sense of well-being, our sense of health, even our sense of beauty to determine who should belong. But that is sinful. "God does not will that I should fashion the other person according to the image that seems good to me, that is, in my own image... rather in his very freedom from me God made this person in His image. I can never know beforehand how God's image should appear in others. That image always manifests a completely new and unique form that comes solely from God's free and sovereign creation" (Bonhoeffer, 1954, 93).

Thus, everyone who lives is an image of the loveliness of God, someone beautiful to God, someone to be prized and cherished. It is not for us to determine how one made in God's image should be; rather, in gratitude and joy we accept all people as beautiful reflections of God whose very existence gives glory to God. In justice we are obliged to see everyone as sacraments of God's presence, manifestations of God's life. As Bonhoeffer says, "To me the sight may seem strange, even ungodly," But God created everyone in the divine image (Bonhoeffer, 1954, 93); if this is true, to reject anyone as unworthy is to make the same decision about God.

CONCLUSION

Carl, the Christmas morning child who took everyone by surprise, is a wonderful, beautiful gift. And he is a sacrament - a revelation of God and a revelation of ourselves. What we have learned in pondering the mystery of this gift, is that we cannot begin to discuss the question of access to the sacraments for persons with developmental disabilities, until we first see clearly what it is persons with disabilities teach us about ourselves and about God. As sacraments of ourselves, they challenge us to rest in our neediness and find power in our helplessness; as sacraments of God, they remind us that the most startling anomaly is not the disabled in our midst, but the love of a God who surpasses everything we would expect. We answer questions about accessibility not when we determine who is healthy and who is not, but when we reflect on God's absolute accessibility.

That tiny child enmeshed in tubes and tape was someone to revere and a cause for awe. What we see now, however, is that what startles us about Carl's existence is not his disability, but the character of the God who lives in him. Ultimately, we learn how to treat the disabled justly when we realise that no one deviates more from our sense of the normal than God, and this is precisely our hope.

Notes

1.   In referring to persons with developmental disabilities as "Sacraments," I am not speaking of the official sacraments of the Church, but indicating how persons with disabilities can reveal something crucial to our understanding of God and our understanding of ourselves that we often overlook. To speak of the developmentally disabled as "sacraments" in this sense in no way denies their need for the redemptive grace of God that comes to us through the sacraments of the Church.

2.   I am grateful to Richard B. Steele for this point and for many other helpful suggestions for this chapter.

Further Reading

Hauerwas, S. (1986). *Suffering Presence*. Notre Dame: University of Notre Dame Press. This is a collection of essays, some of which focus on a theological interpretation of suffering, the moral challenge of persons with developmental disabilities, and a Christian's attitude to the disabled.

McGill, A.C. (1987). *Death and Life: An American Theology*.

Philadelphia: Fortress. This is a challenging and insightful book which examines the dominant understanding of the person in American society in light of an alternative Christian understanding and critique. It is provocative, beautifully written, and often very moving.

Nolan, C. (1987). *Under the Eye of the Clock*. New York: Dell. This brilliant and beautiful autobiographical novel explores the experience of being disabled. There is no better book for capturing not only the challenges which beset persons with developmental disabilities, but also how the world of the able-bodied looks at them.

Acknowledgement

Reproduced from Edward Foley (ed.), (1994). *Developmental Disabilities and Sacramental Access - New Paradigms for Sacramental Encounters*. Collegeville, Minnesota: The Liturgical Press, By kind permission of author and publisher.

REFERENCES

Bonhoeffer, D. (1964). *Life Together*. Trans. John W. Doberstein.
      San Francisco: Harper and Row.
DeRosa, T. (1980). *Paper Fish*. Chicago: The Wine Press.
Green, G. (1971). *The Heart of the Matter*. New York: Penguin Books.
Hauerwas, S. (1977). *Truthfulness and Tragedy*. Notre Dame: University of Notre Dame Press.
Hauerwas, S. (1982). *Suffering Presence*. Notre Dame: University of Notre Dame Press.
McGill, A.C. (1982). *A Test of Theological Method*. Philadelphia: The Westminister Press.
McGill, A.C. (1987). *Death and Life: An American Theology*. Philadelphia: Fortress Press.
Nolan, C. (1987). *Under the Eye of the Clock*. New York: Dell Publishing.
Peck, M. (1990). *A Bed by the Window*. New York: Bantam Books.

Biographical Notes

Paul Wadell, C.P., is associate professor of ethics at Catholic Theological Union in Chicago. He is the author of *Friendship and the Moral Life: An introduction to the Ethics of Thomas Aquinas,* and *Friends of God: Virtues and Gifts in Aquinas*, as well as several articles on Christian ethics and spirituality. He received his Ph.D from the University of Notre Dame.

4 SHARED LEARNING IN COMMUNITIES, CONGREGATIONS AND CHURCHES

Roy McConkey

Social isolation is common for people with intellectual disabilities. In the past, services tended to segregate them from their peers, albeit with the intention of giving them the specialist attention they needed. But as Mark Twain wryly observed; half the results of good intentions are evil and in the case of people labelled as 'mentally handicapped' or 'learning disabled' this has resulted in able-bodied people feeling unable to cope with their disabled peers. Consequently, many are reluctant to become personally involved with individuals who have this disability. Sadly this is just as true for church members.

The essential message of this chapter is that people who have intellectual disability need to be accepted into communities if they are to enjoy a life which is '*as full and as normal as possible*' (to quote a United Nations Declaration of Rights). This is no less true for Christian communities but against the background of social exclusion, which these people have endured in this century, these familiar words of Christ take on a new meaning:

> *There are other sheep which belong to me which are not in this sheepfold. I must bring them too; they will listen to my voice and they will become one flock with one shepherd* (John 10, 16).

Three issues are explored. Firstly, the influences which predispose people to reject people with disabilities and how these can be overcome. Particular attention is paid to the threats posed to a Christian self-image by disability.

Secondly, the contributions which Christian communities can make to the social life of the person who has intellectual disability and the responses required by local congregations to make this more of a reality.

Thirdly, I will argue that the cognitive and emotional dimensions of one's Christianity are underpinned by social relationships and with people who have intellectual disability in particular, our forms of worship and Christian education must take due account of this.

Yet the cardinal message is simply this, the Christian community has to value the contribution which people with disabilities can make to the church and to our society. They too are God's gift to their family and to the world; we have much to learn from them.

One With Us

Humankind has had to contend with disabilities in every society and in every age. They are an invariable part of the human condition. Medical advances may have helped to eliminate many handicapping conditions and modern research promises further preventative actions, but the prospect of a society free of disabled people is an unattainable goal and arguably an undesirable one. There will always be people with disabilities in our communities, congregations and churches.

An essential starting point for our deliberations must be to ask what value disabled people are to our society? For many, the answer is obvious - none at all. Hence, the prevention of disabilities is a priority among Governments and medical researchers, even if it means abortion of 'at risk' as well as damaged foetuses or the withholding of life-sustaining treatments with damaged infants whose prognosis is poor.

Disabled people are commonly viewed as 'takers' rather than 'givers'; they are a drain on their families, on local services and ultimately on tax-payers' money. The life time's care (50 years or more) of a child born in 1998 with a profound disability will easily exceed a million pounds at today's prices.

The 'disaster of disability' has led people to question why a living God permits such suffering and among the faithful, Fervent prayers and pilgrimages to places of healing are common. Indeed the Gospels recount many instances of Jesus removing people's disabilities.

The message is clear whatever perspective you take - disabilities are a curse; seen by various religions as a 'cross to bear' or a punishment for misdeeds in a previous existence. They are no value to a human being or to human society.

BUT, and it is a very big BUT, that is not to say that a person with a disability is valueless. The distinction between the person and the disability is crucial and for those who believe in the concept of the 'soul' (or some related idea) it should be an easy distinction to sustain. Why should bodily imperfections impair the soul?

Seeing the Disability and not the Person

However, humankind is often blind to this distinction. Our feelings of despair and helplessness when confronted with disability make us want to avoid having anything to do with a disabled person. Hence, people with disabilities have been put away into institutions and deprived of an ordinary life. Such actions have been justified as being beneficial to them - '*They are better looked after there*'; '*They are happier with their own kind*' - but the biggest beneficiaries were the able-bodied of society who no longer had to care about their disabled neighbour or relative.

This scenario is re-lived every day. The primary school teacher who wants the slow learner removed to a special class; the employer who cannot find a job for the young man with a physical disability and the clergyman who wishes that the lady who disrupts the services because of her mental illness would worship elsewhere. The solution is always the same; '*I can't cope - put them away.*'

Segregation is so pervasive a response to disability (and to deviancy of any sort) that it makes all the more striking Jesus's emphasis on the inclusiveness of his call - '*Come to me all of you who are tired from carrying heavy loads, and I will give you rest*' (Matt 11: 28).

More than that, He valued the person while they had the disability. Recall the story of the man with leprosy. Jesus did what no other sensible human being would do - he stretched out his hand and *touched* the man with leprosy.

You can never learn to distinguish the person from the disability until you reach out and 'touch' a person who has a disability. It is personal contact that breaks down the barriers and starts to strip away the disability facade so that we discover the person within. Until we start to do this, we can never begin to value their place within our community, congregation or church.

Modern Day Leprosy

People with marked physical or intellectual disability are the modern-day lepers of our society. Parents report a drop-off in the number of people calling to the house when their baby is discovered to have Down Syndrome. Children tease and make fun of the teenager with cerebral palsy. Neighbours protest at the prospect of a home for young adults with an intellectual disability opening in their locality.

According to theories of attitude formation, a person's self-concept is a potent influence on the attitudes they hold of others (Rokeach, 1973). If people feel uncomfortable in the company of people with disabilities - not knowing what to say or how to react, maybe even fearful of a physical attack - then their image of themselves as a competent adult, comes under threat. Avoidance is a prime defensive strategy. Their negative feelings are projected on to the cause of their unease - in this instance the person with the disability.

Creating more positive attitudes, the argument runs, entails making people feel better about themselves and engendering a confidence that they can cope. The key to effective attitude change is NOT more television programmes and newspaper articles about disability. Rather it is through creating enjoyable interactions between the public and people with disabilities. Jesus's example of touching the leper says it all!

A growing body of research evidence highlights the importance of personal contact in changing people's attitudes (McConkey and McCormack, 1983).

Teachers and nursery school leaders reluctant to take children with special needs in their classes were won over when they had experience of doing this for a year. Teenagers from secondary schools viewed people of their own age who had intellectual disability much more positively following an integrated 'club' held in their school. Neighbours who were wary of having a group home open in their locality expressed few concerns or problems two year later after they had opportunities to get to know the people with disabilities.

At the very least then, the churches and their members should be to the fore in reaching out and touching the disabled people in their neighbourhood; welcoming them to their fellowship and providing an example that the wider community can follow. No doubt it is happening, but not to the extent to which it could and should occur.

Indeed, in my more pessimistic moments I wonder if disability poses an even greater threat to the Christian self-image than that experienced by our agnostic neighbours. Church communities may prove even less welcoming as they strive to protect their self-identity. And I don't just mean in terms of access to their buildings although for people with mobility problems, coping with the inevitable steps into church buildings is a formidable obstacle to a warm welcome.

Threats to a Christian Self-Image

Intellectual disability, seems to me to pose particular challenges to Christians.

- *'I'm supposed to love them but I can't'* - As men and women strive to follow Christ's teaching, they find it hard to overcome their natural reactions. Avoidance becomes even more appealing to them. Similar reactions can be found among other people in society - such as doctors and schoolteachers - who might be expected to be able to cope with disability but who personally find it hard. Some of the most negative reactions recounted by people with disabilities and their parents feature professionals who might have been expected to help.

- *'Do I sin by association?'* - Folk myths of people being possessed by evil spirits may linger longer than we care to admit. Equally, the villain in fairy stories or in modern-day film and television dramas is frequently depicted with deformities. The old Levitical teaching may also implicitly influence the thinking of some church members -

> *No one who is blind, lame, disfigured or deformed: no one with a crippled hand or foot; no one who is a hunchback or a dwarf; no one with an eye or skin disease and no eunuch... may present the food-offering to me ... Because he has a physical defect, he shall not come near the sacred curtain or approach the altar (Lev 21:18-20, 23).*

- *Why does a loving God allow disabilities?* - Like doctors, the Christian community does not wish to be reminded of its 'failures' and apparent lack of latter-day miracle healings. Indeed, the churches are still striving to formulate a theology of suffering and the attempts of modern theologians rarely merit a mention in Sunday homilies and sermons.

- *How can people with a disability make a commitment like mine?* The 'holier than you' mentality is hard to avoid, especially with people with an intellectual disability who apparently have an imperfect grasp of Christian beliefs. If we admit them to full membership of the church and the Sacraments, are we not devaluing the thoughtful commitments of others? This argument is particularly potent with those responsible for admitting, or rather not admitting, people to full church membership.

  The Pharisees of Jesus's day must have had similar feelings towards the people who Jesus chose as his disciples - illiterate, uneducated fishermen who if tested on the intelligence tests of today might well come out as having intellectually disability.

- *Can people with disabilities minister to me?* The dearth of people with disabilities among clergy and laity in positions of leadership, reinforces the image of 'perfection' which the old Leviticus laws stressed. But more crucially the concept of people with disabilities ministering to others rather than the more usual role of being ministered to, is so alien to our culture and way of living that it verges on the unthinkable (Monteith, 1987).

Some would argue that other groups in society have been equally marginalised by the churches and effectively debarred from ministering to others – women and coloured immigrants. Our tendency to create God in our own image is challenged by the feminist assertion that God is female. Can we conceive of a God who is disabled? Recall the words of our Lord,

Whenever you did this for one of the least important of these brothers of mine, you did it for me. (Matt 25,40)

Christian Communities

Forgive me if I have painted an unnecessarily gloomy and overly pessimistic view of the churches' involvement with people who have disabilities. The point I want to emphasise is simply this – churches have colluded with the social exclusion practices of secular society . But those practices are now disappearing fast.

An increasing number of children with disabilities attend mainstream schools; many school-leavers with intellectual disabilities go on work experience placements with local businesses, and people from long-stay mental handicap hospitals are being re-settled into community houses. Within every parish or congregational district of 5,000 people there are likely to be upwards of 50 people with some form of intellectual disability. At the very least they must be included as part of the church's outreach into the community.

But more than this, churches can contribute significantly to making 'community care policies' a success and I would argue that they are potentially well placed to do this.

The parish or congregational structure can offer a range of opportunities from the cradle to the grave. Figure 1 lists these from the birth of the baby with a disability.

Figure 1. Social opportunities often provided by Churches

Birth of the baby
> Family support
> Baptism
> Crèche
> Mother and Toddler Groups
> Nursery/Playgroup
> Sunday School
> Youth Organisations and Clubs
> Confirmation Classes
> Outings / retreats / weekend holidays
> Sports - Badminton, Bowls
> Choir - Musical societies; hobby clubs
> Young women's/men's groups
> Bible study / prayer groups
> Home fellowships
> Care groups such as meals on wheels
> Senior Citizen Groups
> Church committees

Or special schemes can be developed to address the particular needs of people with disabilities. The Faith and Light movement inspired by Jean Vanier is one example (see chapter 11 by Bob Brooke in this volume) and others are provided in the book edited by Kelly and McGinley, 1990.

A number of points are worth emphasising.

• Social integration has to start as soon as the disability is recognised. Colleagues of mine have offered training to clergy in approaching and supporting families after a diagnosis of a disability has been made; a role for which many feel inadequately prepared. This offer of fellowship and solidarity can set the tone for the child's engagement with the wider community as well as encouraging the family to bring the child forward for baptism.

- As noted above, the child and family's social integration can be further fostered through the range of activities provided by many congregations but this is more likely to occur when leaders and helpers are prepared to plan for, and to give extra attention to the member with disabilities and when some members from the group 'befriend' the person with the disability. Some youth organisations such as the Scouts have training officers who can advise local leaders in this area (May, 1987).

- The ceremonies we use to mark people's maturing – baptism, confirmation and communion – are just as important, if not more important for people with disabilities and for their families. Preparation for these can form a useful goal for our religious education (McClorry, 1990).

- Positions of leadership and responsibility must be open to people with disabilities according to their talents. They may need special help and extra preparation in undertaking these roles, but such assistance could benefit all who assume positions of leadership (Bowers, 1988).

One of my favourite disability stories in the New Testament is of the men who brought the paralysed man to the crowded house where Jesus was teaching and ended up making a hole in the roof; lowering him down on his mat so that he ended up at Jesus's feet.

Here in a nutshell is the congregational response to people with disabilities. The paralysed man needed *friends* to ensure that he didn't miss out on what was going on in Capernaum.

The friends were not easily defeated. Their *ingenuity* created another way of getting the man to Jesus when the usual method didn't work.

Above all, Jesus was moved by the *faith* shown by the friends. They are all heroes of this story. How much faith have we that disabled people are worth the effort to bring them to Jesus?

The congregation who learns to care will inevitably influence the wider community as the members go about their everyday life in neighbourhoods, work places and social events. It is hypocritical of church folk to decry the lack of community caring while doing nothing to promote greater social integration among themselves.

Christian Education

Social relationships are important for another reason. Religious knowledge and understanding is inextricably linked with humankind's superior cognitive development and competence in symbolic thinking. We have as yet a very imperfect understanding of how children acquire these competencies. In the last decade, though, a revolution has occurred in psychological thinking about children's cognitive development.

For years, researchers and indeed educators, have treated children as immature islands, complete unto themselves. Rudolf Schaffer (1987) put it this way,

> Most accounts of psy*chological development have been individual-based, their concern has been with the child as such, everything outside has skin being considered extraneous.*

A high emphasis was therefore placed on genetic endowments in explaining differences in children's intellectual abilities and a teacher's role was to 'pour in' knowledge to the empty vessels. To this day, it is their efforts which form the corpus of educational psychology studied - and endured - by aspiring teachers.

Modern thinking has changed radically. It is best summed up by Schaffer's assertion that, *'Human development is fundamentally a joint enterprise between child and caretakers.'* The implications of this, he saw as follows,

Cognitive functions require a social context for their initial emergence and subsequent facilitation before they eventually become internalised as properties of individuals.

To concretise his assertion even further, you might care to substitute the following phrases for "cognitive functions" - expressive language or even moral judgements.

To study a child's cognitive growth in isolation of his or her natural interactors is to see only half the picture at best; a distorted image at worst. Put simply, children's earliest cognitive skills only exist during interactions with people to whom they are in 'tune'. And although the physical maturing of the infant may have some contribution to make, the birth of cognitive processes is stimulated and supported by the knowledgeable interactor.

The implications are even greater though for teachers; those parents and professionals wishing to promote children's understandings. Jerome Bruner (1972) expressed it thus,

> *One of the most crucial ways in which culture provides aids in intellectual growth is through a **dialogue** between the more experienced and the less experienced.*

Yet in educational settings, the 'lecture' is more common than the dialogue. Tizard and Hughes (1984) contrasted children's conversations at home with those they had with teachers at nursery schools. They wrote of the latter,

> *The kind of dialogue that seems to help children is not that currently favoured by many teachers in which the adult poses a series of questions. Rather it is one in which the adult listens to the child's questions and comments, helps to clarify her ideas, and feeds her the information she asks for.*

Lev Vygotsky (1978) spelt out other conditions which apply to all cognitive tasks, although in this instance he is focusing on one,

*Writing should be **meaningful** for children, an intrinsic need should be aroused in them and that writing should be incorporated into a task that is necessary and meaningful for (their) life.*

Margaret Donaldson, in her influential book, *Children's Minds* (1978) summarised the 'very important part of the job of a teacher', as being,

...to guide the child towards tasks where he will be able objectively to do well, but not too easily, not without putting forth some effort, not without difficulties to be mastered, errors to be overcome, creative solutions to be found.

Handling evidence and solving one's own problems are essential to cognitive maturity.

The three attributes - dialogue, meaning and success – needed to nurture mental growth, appear to me to feature insufficiently in many of the approaches used in Christian education. A high reliance is placed on 'preaching' rather than dialogue; on abstractions rather than application and on 'received wisdom' rather than self-discovery.

Once again in Christ we have a model for religious education; a model that is especially pertinent for people with special educational needs. Disabilities were much more common among the people to whom He proclaimed the gospel and by comparison with modern society, many of the able-bodied then would today be labelled slow learners!

Christ relied on the parable – a story of daily life, to reveal a deeper truth in a way that was meaningful to his listeners. The Gospels recount many of Christ's dialogues - from the age of twelve in the Temple to His trial with Pilate. And He left people to make up their own minds about Him, be it the rich young ruler or his trusted disciple, Simon Peter.

But above all, He gave us the example of the teacher sharing in the life of the learners as He toured the towns and villages of Galilee. Not for Him the distance-learning course in Theology!

Recreating this model in churches and schools is not easy. Families come much closer to the ideal. Parental involvement in the education of children with special needs is one of the great success stories of the past two decades. What resources and training can we offer parents in the field of Christian education?

And when families are unable or unwilling to undertake this, what style of educational input do we make? Activity based learning within small friendship groups led by a responsive tutor who can provide opportunities for one-to-one attention appear to be the most promising educational *milieu* for the special needs child even if it is not always the most practical within schools (Harris, 1993).

I see two formidable obstacles however to this approach. First, it is dependent on a tutor who is willing and confident enough to share his or her faith in response to the learner's enquiries. Second, there is a danger of heretical teaching as personal opinions replace the accepted doctrines of the church. Of course neither of these obstacles are peculiar to religious education for people with special needs and the solution lies in the wider education and support that is offered to all church members.

Religious Beliefs

Unlike other educational subjects, religious education has to embrace the emotions as well as cognitions. Indeed for many believers, their faith is an emotional rather than an intellectual experience. Christian churches, especially those in the Calvinistic tradition have been wary of encouraging emotional expression. Some would claim that this is reflected in the national stereotypes of the British and other North Europeans compared with the Latin temperaments of the Italians and Spanish.

People with disabilities rarely suffer from impaired emotions. Even the person with the most severe mental and physical disability can experience happiness and sadness; show anger and affection; be anxious and relaxed. If their disabilities are such that we cannot reach them on an intellectual level, then we must use the emotions. The programme created by the Special Religious Education Division (SPRED) of the Roman Catholic Archdiocese of Chicago offers excellent examples as to how this can be done through shared worship which uses symbols and sensations to enhance the emotional experience for the participants (Harrington, 1990).

Some of these approaches would, I believe, enrich religious education for everyone. Our Christian communities often do not reflect the idea of 'togetherness' inherent in the Greek word *"Koinonia"*, which, I gather, embodied the idea of a fellowship for mutual benefit and good in the widest sense of the term. It was used of the marriage relationship; business partnerships, and is the very essence and foundation of friendship (Barclay, 1967). In all these instances, it is shared emotions which forge the sense of togetherness.

Which brings me back to my starting point, namely what contribution can people with disabilities make to our church and to our communities?

Brendan Kelly (1988) argues that people with an intellectual disability, *'can have a real gift for the Church in the ecumenical area.'* In sharing our beliefs with them, we are forced to come back to the basics of our faith and in so doing we emphasise what we have in common and not what divides us.

But perhaps God is working a wider good through people with disabilities. They show none of the qualities which advanced societies treasure - intelligence, initiative, self-sufficiency and good looks. But during my twenty-five years of working in this field I have been struck by how people with disabilities, their families and the staff who care for them are all forced to live their lives by another set of values - compassion, kindness, gentleness and patience. Thus, the very presence of a person with disabilities in our midst keeps alive the fruits of the spirit of which Paul wrote. In this respect, modern society more than ever needs people with disabilities to remind them of what it means to be human.

Equally, the person with disabilities who experiences these values in action is more likely to be given opportunities to participate more fully and equitably within our society. And arguably we provide the highest form of religious education as we demonstrate these qualities in our own lives.

Christopher Nolan (1987), the gifted Irish writer who is so physically disabled that he cannot talk and has no control over any of his movements and is thus totally dependent on others, had this to say of the teachers who took time to discover the meanings he tried to convey through his facial expressions, eye movements and body language.

> *It was moments such as these that Joseph (himself) recognised the face of God in human form. It glimmered in their kindness to him, it glowed in their keenness, it hinted in their caring, indeed it caressed in their gaze.*

What higher aspiration can there be for these who profess to be Christian than to show to our fellow citizens with disabilities the face of God.

REFERENCES

Barclay, W. (1967). *The Plain Man looks at the Apostle's Creed .* London: Fontana.

Bowers, F. (1988). *Who is this sitting in my pew? Mentally handicapped people in the Church.* London: Triangle/SPCK.

Bruner, J. (1972). *The Relevance of Education.* London: Allen and Unwin.

Donaldson, M. (1978). *Children's Minds.* London: Fontana.

Harrington, M.T. (1990). Special Religious Education: SPRED Chicago. In B. Kelly and P. McGinley, (eds), *Mental Handicap: Challenge to the Church.* Chorley, Lancashire: Lisieux Hall.

Harris, J. (1993). *Innovations in Educating Children with Severe Learning Difficulties.* Chorley, Lancashire: Lisieux Hall.

Kelly, B. (1988). People with mental handicap and the Church: Gift and Call. In R. McConkey and P. McGinley (eds), *Concepts and Controversies in Services for People with a Mental Handicap.* Galway: Woodlands Centre.

Kelly, B. & McGinley, P. (1990). Mental Handicap: *Challenge to the Church.* Chorley, Lancashire: Lisieux Hall.

McConkey, R. and McCormack, B. (1983). *Breaking Barriers: Educating people about disability.* London: Souvenir Press.

McClorry, J. (1990) In B. Kelly and P. McGinley, (eds), *Mental Handicap: Challenge to the Church.* Chorley, Lancashire: Lisieux Hall.

McConkey, R. and Price, P. (1986). *Let's Talk: Learning language in everyday settings*. London: Souvenir Press.

May, R. (1987). *Let's Integrate: Young people with handicaps in youth organisations.* Sutton: Printforce.

Monteith, W.G. (1987). *Disability: Faith and Acceptance.* Edinburgh: St Andrew Press.

Nolan, C. (1987). *Under the Eye of the Clock.* London: Pan Books.

Rokeach, M. (1973). *The Nature of Human Values*. New York: Free Press.

Schaffer, H.R. (1986). Child psychology: The future. *Journal of Child Psychology and Psychiatry,* 27, 761-779.

Tizard, B. and Hughes, M. (1984). *Young Children Learning: Talking and thinking at home and playschool.* London: Fontana.

Vygotsky, L. (1978). *Mind and Society: The Development of Higher Psychological Process.* Cambridge, Mass: Harvard University Press.

Biographical Note

Roy McConkey is Professor of Learning Disability, University of Ulster, a post he took up in 1997. During the previous ten years, he worked for the Brothers of Charity Services in the Borders Region of Scotland. An Ulster Presbyterian by upbringing, he has latterly been an elder in the Church of Scotland and leader of a Faith & Light community in Galashiels.

5 AFFECTIVITY AND SYMBOL IN THE PROCESS OF CATECHESIS

Mary Therese Harrington, S.H.

Catechesis comes in many shapes and sizes. Like a garment of great value, it has to fit each person. When a person has a developmental disability that entails mental limitations, the catechesis has to be carefully crafted. The fabric of catechesis is the same from generation to generation, but the core of the Christian mystery needs to be approached in a subtle and sensitive manner with those who have developmental disabilities, whether they be children, adolescents, or adults.

The core of the good news is that the merciful love of God is manifest in Jesus. It is treasured in the people of God who live in the love of the Holy Spirit who leads all back to God. This care has been approached in various ways not only from generation to generation, but from culture to culture and now with new awareness from disability to disability. I want to focus on those who have significant mental limitations. In our relationships with them, they push us to our limits. And as we struggle with those with disabilities and they struggle with us, some valuable insights can be gained. The two most valuable insights for me that have come from this mutual struggle are the role of affectivity in catechesis and the need to develop a symbolic consciousness.

Affectivity in Catechesis

Faith education is not the same as transmission of knowledge. Faith education, catechesis, involves an awakening to the mystery that we are loved by a merciful God. It is a call to relate. One authentically relates with affectivity, be it positive or negative. Affectivity is the ability to feel and to express emotions.

It is different from intelligence and will, but just as fundamental to the well-being of a person.

One can consider affectivity as background to faith or as foreground in the process of "doing" faith. As *background*, affectivity makes up the faith world into which a person is invited to enter. Since the mystery of faith is the tenderness with which God gazes on us, the role of the catechist is to give witness to this tenderness. The witness is given through the gaze of the catechist. With a person who cannot speak and is slow to respond to spoken language, the call is through one's eyes. With one who refuses to look, the invitation is through a slow process of sitting side by side until a look can be exchanged, a breakthrough experienced, a relationship initiated. The catechist takes the initiative because of familiarity with the tenderness of God.

As background, affectivity includes the sounds that one chooses to make part of an ambience. It includes the scents of flowers, of warm bread, of cocoa. It includes the light and warmth in a room. It means that everything that is impersonal, harsh, institutional (like a traditional classroom) is avoided. Affectivity includes the whole person who sets out to lead a person with a disability on the journey of faith (i.e., the catechist, the sponsor). As a catechist, one has to tune one's own affectivity as one tunes the strings of a violin before entering into the music that is catechesis. One has to situate one's own affectivity. It is not just a question of forcing oneself to be in a certain mood. Rather, it is a question of positioning oneself to be flexible, receptive, warm, open, and totally hospitable.

The awareness out of which we move in the act of catechesis is our sense of the tenderness and compassion with which God offers us friendship and salvation. In turn, we as catechists approach our friends with the tenderness and compassion that offers friendship. The source of the love with which we love our friends is the love with which God loves us. To get in touch with this mystery, we obviously need some time and space to ourselves before we meet a person for catechesis.

Above and beyond knowing the general outline of what we want to do, we want to be aware of our own feelings. Are we dry, sad, in turmoil? Are we angry, upset, cranky? If we are convinced that our friends quickly pick up our affect and that we may be a block or a blessing to them, we become adept at fine tuning ourselves, that is, we work on our ability to feel and to express emotion. For some, this fine tuning happens through listening to a favourite piece of music. Others keep clay handy, twenty minutes with clay and they are ready. Others sit still and breathe deeply in a structured bodily position. Others go for a short walk. The point of the exercise is to clear one's head and one's heart to be available on a deep level.

Affectivity as background means also a grasp of the role affect plays in the lives of those with developmental disabilities. When a person with a disability is afraid and hesitant, the intellectual functioning that they do have is impaired. When they are relaxed and peaceful, their intellectual functioning is improved. When there is an ambience of reassurance, there is a liberation of energy.

How often a child with normal mental capacity who is insecure or in anguish is mistaken for a child with mental retardation! If this poor state continues over time, the child actually will become mentally retarded because the whole organism is blocked in its development. A child can thus become developmentally disabled. On the other hand, when a child is surrounded by adults who respect, love and cherish him or her, even if there is brain damage or slow mental development for genetic reasons, the child thrives according to what ever capacity is possible. One cheers for the child, adolescent, young adult or adult struggling to construct him - or herself with courage and hope. One offers all the support possible to shore up a fragile equilibrium.

Any developing person needs a great deal of love and reassurance to get over the hard spots of life. As youngsters with a disability become conscious of how they are different, they struggle with their self-image. They can be demanding, capricious, moody, and angry. Some can go through periods when all affectivity seems to have atrophied and they appear much more disabled than they actually are. Others break loose in a superabundance of affectivity.

Catechists who are aware of the primordial role of affectivity in themselves and in the development of the person with a disability still have to become comfortable with the role of affectivity in catecheses itself.

Affectivity is not the same as being sentimental. It does not mean that all one has to do with people with disabilities is to love or pity them. Nor is affectivity in catechesis something of which one should be afraid. One hopes that catechesis is entered into by mature adults who are aware of their own emotions and those of our friends with disabilities. Being aware is a large part of this catechesis.

Since it is impossible to enter into the catechetical act without affectivity, the question is its quality. The quality of the affectivity is determined by the quality of the relationships. Relationships are possible with a person with a disability, even if the disability is severe and profound. Unless a person is in a coma, there is some relating going on, since they have agreed to live. The art form of catechesis is to relate to the person in order to awaken their feelings, to help them to develop a friendship and then within that friendship to venture on the journey of faith development. Naturally, this is a delicate and beautiful process.

Building bonds of friendship with those who have mental limitations is an adventure. One finds oneself looking forward to moments together because they are marked by sincerity, simplicity, pleasure, and the authenticity of mutual affection. This is as it should be. One has to look forward with desire to relationships if one is to persevere in them. However, the positive aspects of a relationship may be a distant goal to be pursued by the catechist as well as the person with the disability. A phase of negative or false relating is possible. One can spot it by the lack of confidence, spontaneity, and creativity in those involved. A struggle is in process. Both the person with a disability and the catechist need room for their own struggles with the process of conversion. Just because a phase is hard, one does not give up the process. One struggles on in hope of a breakthrough.

In a difficult phase, or in a negative relationship, there can be unreal expectations and manipulation on both sides. One can only wait to see how the drama will unfold. Sometimes the relationship has to be cut to allow escape before there is damage done.

INNOCENCE

Vincent and Joyce have one child, Francisco, who is mildly retarded. Francisco attends special classes at a nearby public school. His parents approached their parish priest to ask if Francisco might be prepared for his first confession. In their former parish, several years before, a kind teacher had tried to give Francisco a few instructions and the parish priest had permitted him to make his first Communion. The pastor of their new parish is known to be very kind. He told Vincent and Joyce that they should not worry: God knows, he assured them, that an "innocent, handicapped child" like Francisco would never do anything wrong for which he would be responsible. Confession, the pastor insisted, was not necessary for Francisco.

In an ambiguous relationship, the catechist may want to feel good about relating to a particular person with a disability. But unless this person is loved for her or his own sake, such an adventure will be tested, tried, and found wanting. There will be no opening in catechesis, no breakthrough, because affectivity is not flowing in the right direction. The faith growth of the person with a disability can be blocked by catechists whose main motive is their egocentric need to feel good about themselves.

Affectivity in catechesis is disciplined and demanding. It has tensions, conflicts, reconciliations and breakthroughs. But its purpose is to help individuals with a disability to situate themselves in relation to others and to God. It is to help them to grow, to conquer their fears and dependency. It is a chance to conquer the autonomy that they can achieve.

How does one persevere in this drama? One needs to work with a team of catechists. The team reflects on relationships with kindness and compassion. Strategies are developed; plans are shared. Feedback is respectfully given and gratefully received.

Against this backdrop, we can now consider affectivity as an element in the *foreground* in the act of catechesis. Up front, as it were, the catechist masters language. The first thing to master is to speak in the first and second person ("I" - "you"). Third person language ("it - "they") will never have much impact on a person with significant intellectual disabilities. Dialogue always has to be in direct address.

Next, one frequently speaks the name of the person with feeling in one's voice. This affirms that I am speaking to you. I know you. I acknowledge you. I call you to respond. Even in a small group, one avoids using "we" until each person feels noticed, affirmed, included, valued, and cherished.

If a person seems lost or confused, I stop to speak of what I feel. I speak of what you may feel. I try to clarify some obscurity that seems to have blocked or put a lid on the flow of communications. The flow has to continue if one is to bring a person to a moment of praise or gratitude.

Catechesis is only possible with those who have significant developmental disabilities if they feel themselves to be loved. This affectivity is the gate to their comprehension of who God is for them. One works so hard on relationships because the quality of the relationship allows the other person to discover that relating to God is possible.

Within a group of six persons with developmental disabilities and their six sponsors (one sponsor for each), the catechist works to support a whole network of relationships. Our being together is meant to build church here and now among us. The essential mystery of which we hope to become more aware depends for its roots on our own relationships in our own little community of faith. It is thus that the small group becomes a privileged place for personal and faith growth. There is no competition. Each one struggles to grow according to their own capacity. Amazing gestures of love and affection are offered and accepted. Signs of concern and support multiply. Help is freely given and freely received.

In this ambience, one can proclaim the merciful love of God. Until this ambience is achieved, it is difficult to proclaim the good news. Naturally, with this process, communities have to stay together for a period of time. Moving from grade to grade would be counterproductive. It takes time to build relationships of quality.

The Good News can be communicated in an abstract, highly conceptual, and dry manner with those who have normal intellectual functioning. It may do nothing to awaken faith. If the recipients are well brought up, they will sit and take it; however, they may drop out of the scene later on. If one tries to go the abstract way with those with mental disabilities, one is simply talking to oneself. If affectivity is avoided, how can faith be transmitted?

The Holy Spirit lives in each person, no matter the extent of their disability. And so there is one at work in the heart of the person before I as a catechist ever arrive on the scene. My work is to be in touch with the Holy Spirit within myself and thus be sensitive to work on the level at which catechesis achieves its purpose; one says the word and there is a resonance, an echo in the heart of the one who responds. This is the truest description of catechesis which we have received from the early Church.

Symbolic Awareness

The structure of symbol merits some attention before reflecting on developing a symbolic awareness. Symbolic activity always involves having a kind of double vision. One is in touch at the same time with a *here and now* phenomenon and a *beyond* phenomenon. One must keep them in tension and in balance; sad things can happen if this balance is lost.

A psychological way to look at symbol is to see the two poles as an outer and inner vision. Imagine persons very much involved in their own inner world, so much so that this inner world takes up all their attention. They may hear inner voices, they may talk to themselves, they may respond primarily to inner stimuli that no one else can perceive. We see such persons as having an emotional problem. They have lost touch with their outer vision.

On the other hand, imagine persons living totally in the outer, impersonal world. They do not reflect on what is happening to them. They are not aware of what they think or what they feel. Since they are not sensitive to themselves, they may be ill at ease with others who may need attention. We see such persons as having a superficial life. They have lost touch with their inner vision.

For the person who tilts toward a totally inner world, religion is a subjective, interior mystery. But when the focus is on the surface reality, mystery can become a kind of religious magic. Well-balanced symbolic awareness allows one to keep the everyday world and its religious significance in place. This balance between what we live and its significance is the goal of educating a person in symbolic awareness.

One presumes that God is at work not only in history in its largest sense, but also in our own histories. If God is at work today, and if I am to become aware of this, I first of all have to be aware of what I live in my own life. Then, given the way in which God has acted in the past, I become aware of traces of God's action in the present, in my life.

Persons with normal intellectual functioning can learn about God's intervention in time and space and how other people have become the people of God. Persons with limited intellectual functioning cannot interpret the past. They can only interpret the present because they lack the ability to cope with historical time. Having a historical sense requires a certain level of intellectual functioning. A person who is intellectually limited may not be able to cope with numbers or time. So five days ago, five hundred days ago, five hundred years ago, or five millennia ago may have no felt meaning. One is faced then with working out a synthesis that can be grasped in a global, symbiotic way. Because it is a synthesis, it is no less true than an analysis of history. So, one talks about how God acts more than about how God has acted.

Although a person with mental limitations may lack a historical sense, most have the capacity for symbolic functioning in the sense of early childhood development (mental age of two or three years). This kind of symbolic functioning has two aspects that are helpful in faith education.

First, such persons see things, persons, and events as totally related to themselves. This kind of egocentric functioning is not a moral fault but a phase of intellectual development. Everything of importance is "mine". The tree outside the window is mine, the moon is mine, the squirrel is mine. The advantage of this mode of knowing is that God is totally for them. This is far different from persons who admit the existence of God as an impersonal force who could not possibly be interested in them. Second, such persons have a capacity to be symbolically creative. Suppose the child sees a broom. He or she does not want to manipulate it as a broom but wants to ride it as a horse. The broom has been given a new meaning beyond its first level of meaning. Once a person can cope with a surface event, person, or thing and a secondary level of meaning or significance, there is symbolic functioning that is open to faith education.

This symbolic functioning is different from the way we relate to sign. We learn signs. A stop sign has one meaning and we have to learn that meaning. There is a one-to-one correspondence between the surface reality and the significance. With symbolic awareness, the secondary level of meaning is global and imprecise. One gradually becomes aware of something on the level of insight. With knowledge of signs, learning is objective and impersonal. With symbolic awareness, on the other hand, there is a subjective personal attraction or aversion in an encounter with something beyond the ordinary. Symbolic awareness always involves affectivity.

The structure of symbol also requires one to be sensitive to the positive and negative valences in symbolic awareness. One can slip from one to the other rapidly. Suppose one is looking at a lit candle. If one relates to it symbolically, one enters into a kind of dialogue with it. One takes time with this dialogue. Gradually, the visible, tangible candle, while still being there, awakens a memory. This awakening is spontaneous. It is just there - a kind of evocation that brings with it vague stirrings. One flashes to a pleasant fireplace and on to the memory of the house next door that burned down. One evocation is positive and the other is negative.

Very often in working symbolically with people who are limited in their development, one has to stop to allow for this interplay of positive and negative before one can freeze a frame to move on in a symbolic progression. One starts to evoke new life but has to stop to consider that someone in the group had a goldfish that died. One starts to evoke being in the light, but stops to consider the difficulty someone has with going to sleep in the dark. One tries to move into the evocation of a person who get better but first we have to consider everyone we have ever known who died!

This normal fluctuation between the positive and the negative aspects of symbol is the stuff that develops imagination. It is a glorious event when a person with limitations starts to stumble around in this creative world. When a symbolic progression is achieved, the frame is held, the evocation is steadied, and we start to focus on how we feel with new life (having escaped death), with light (after having slept in the dark), with getting better (after not having died). The person who can move through this evocation of a lived event and can name or assent to having another name for their feelings is ready to respond to catechesis.

If a person lacks the ability for deductive or inductive reasoning (mental age about 12 to 14), one does not set out to *explain* the content of faith. One asserts, one proclaims, one juxtaposes aspects of our faith with aspects of everyday life. By placing everyday life and the significance of faith side by side, a new global, symbolic awareness takes place. Eventually this develops into one's own vision of faith.

For example, suppose we talk about being in the sunlight. We talk about how it feels hot and thirsty, getting sunburned and people getting heatstroke! Then we go back to how good it is to be in the sunlight. We talk about feeling warm and contented. We then move on to our liturgical evocation which we place alongside this first evocation from everyday life. In this session we talk about our Easter liturgy. We focus on a real, live liturgy that we have been at together on a particular day in a particular place. We all sang... and there was a beautiful large candle...

The work thus far may have taken forty minutes. Now we can go on to the biblical evocation. We might solemnly pick up the Scriptures and read several times, "Jesus said, I am the light of the world; anyone who follows me will not be walking in the dark but will have the light of life" (John 8:12). There is silence - no commentary.

Then I, as the leader, would go to each person and the sponsor sitting alongside, to give a kind of blessing. I would put my hands on their heads or, depending on the session, take their hands and say something like, "Robert, today Jesus says to you, I am your light". At the end of the blessing, there would be silence and finally a song that we had sung in a liturgical setting that we can sing by heart. Finally, there might be some quiet music while the symbolic progression falls into place within each person.

In this kind of catechesis, using the French *Method Vivre* (see references), the leader is not so much an instructor as a coach. Each person has to do his or her own work. Each one grows in the process of verbal or gesture expression. Each one learns to express what they live and what it means. But they can do their own work of hermeneutics only if they are led, little by little, and given the vocabulary, the gestures, the ambience, and the community to support their newly formed faith awareness.

In order for such a progression to take place, there are some prerequisites. Sufficient time and a well-prepared place are essential. Contrary to what some believe - that because a person has a short attention span, one should be brief and hurry - one should rather be very deliberate and well paced. I would not begin a catechesis unless I had an hour and forty-five minutes to two hours to work. Individuals will fade in and fade out. That is normal. But when one is working in a symbolic manner, one has to allow time to settle down. One has to allow time for each person to feel what we are talking about. One has to allow time for breakthroughs in relationships and insights. One has to allow time to rest in what we do.

A well-prepared place is essential. That means not only having the proper materials at hand but also having spaces and objects of beauty. One has to love a place as well as the people in it to grow symbolically.

In such a place, with time to work, one needs well-prepared catechists or sponsors who know how to relate and who know that even with the most disabled person, we will work as a team toward four goals.

First, we will work together to develop a sense of the sacred, a sense of mystery. This implies that we approach one another as sacred. We respect one another and show it in how we speak, gesture, and move. We have a room or a corner for our symbolic progression that has the Scriptures in a special place, with fresh flowers and a candle to light. We will have only beautiful music in this space. After time in such a space for faith education we can easily move to liturgical space for worship.

Reverence will not be forced because it will have become part of the person's manner of being. Silence will not be imposed because the person will have had an education in silence. Singing will not be strained because music will be an authentic expression.

Second, we will work together to develop a sense of the people of God. We will begin by building a community of faith among ourselves. We will express our faith together. Together we will participate in the larger assembly's Eucharistic celebrations. We will set time aside to celebrate the sacrament of reconciliation and the major feasts of the year. We will go back to our small groups to relish what happened in the larger assembly.

Third, we will work together to develop a sense of Christ. We know that when we are happy to be together, we can proclaim the presence of Jesus. In each of our sessions, we work to come to the moment when we can hear the message of Jesus. What we do to form bonds of friendship is not just to draw those with disabilities to ourselves but to lead them to the point where, letting go of our hands, they can themselves move toward God in faith.

Fourth, we will work together to develop this movement toward God in faith, hope, and love. In each of our sessions together, we want to enter into some aspect of the mystery of the triune God where the bonds of love are such that there is but one God. We build bonds of love and friendship as a witness to that mystery and as access to participation in that mystery of Trinitarian life.

We have seen that those with disabilities are quite capable of faith education, provided that there is affectivity in abundance and that there is time, space, people, and a process that can develop symbolic competence.

Acknowledgement

Reproduced from Edward Foley (ed.), *Developmental Disabilities and Sacramental Access - New Paradigms for Sacramental Encounters*. Liturgical Press, By kind permission of author and publisher.

Further Reading

Brodeur, R. and others (1989). *La Dynamique Symbolique*. Quebec: Universite Laval. See chapter 6 for more information on the *Method Vivre*.

Brunot, B. *"Affectivité et Relation en Catechese"*. *Lumen Vitea* 46, no. 2, 155-63. Affectivity is an essential element of catechesis.

Cousins, E.H. (1977). *Bonaventure and the Coincidence of Opposites*. Chicago: Franciscan Herald Press. This text is helpful to develop a sense of the structure of symbol.

Harrington, M.T. (1992). *A Place For All - Mental Retardation, Catechesis and Liturgy*. Collegeville: The Liturgical Press. Presents an overview of pastoral action.

Kelly, B. (1990). *Mental Handicap: Challenge to the Church*. Lancashire, England: Brothers of Charity. See chapter 11 for an orientation to the sacraments of initiation with those   who have developmental disabilities.

Biographical Note

Mary Therese Harrington, S.H., is a member of the Chicago Archdiocesan Pastoral Team for Special Religious Education (SPRED). She is a practising catechist with adolescents who have a wide range of developmental disabilities.

6 L'ARCHE

David Wilson

I wake before my alarm goes off.
Ten minutes to listen to the wind.
Another day. Another storm.
I slide out onto my knees.
'Lord. I commend my life into your hands this day.'

Outside it's dry, but blowing hard.
I'm in the Oratory by 6.45 am.
Prayer before Jesus in the Blessed Sacrament.
There are four of us together, maybe five.
I can't be sure.
But we're here together in the presence of the Lord
who made us.

**And the Word became Bread and dwelt
among us, full of grace and truth.**

The Bread of Heaven, Icon of the Father.
Could any presence be simpler, more available?
Such is his longing to be with us.
'Jesus, with you I want to say "yes" to the Father.'

The thoughts of the day ahead come swirling in.
I try to lift them up and into
the Everlasting hands.
Time to go. I give the blessing.
Blessing those present, I also bless
the whole community:

six houses, the workshops, the offices and
services, the families,
about 140 people, 45 with a mental handicap
for whom this is home,
and 30 for whom it is their place of work by day.

Back in the house where I live breakfast has started.
I'm scarcely in the door.
'Père David. Oh Père David.'
Hubert's voice, his face, the whole movement
of his body say:
'Welcome. It's good to see you.'
He continues:
'Today, La Colombe, Peel the potatoes. Foam.
Medal. Pizza. Petit Café.'
He has his day all lined up.
'I am happy.'
To see him and to hear him,
I feel life flow through me.
It's a good feeling.

**I came that they may have life,
and have it abundantly.**

Hubert's favourite music is
Beethoven and Mozart.
I see no fear in him, only openness.
Total truthfulness. Nothing to hide.
Just share what you are, simply.

Jeanne is talking away, talking away,
talking away.
Repeating, intruding. Not easy to accept.
She's tolerated for a while, then Mariethé
tells her to stop.
The others come down.
Paul, quiet and calm, so distinguished

with his beard.
If only his parents would leave him alone,
He feels they are trying to control his life.
Gerard slow, but precise.
Marie-Giles gets a bowl for Odile;
Odile can only walk with difficulty.
People help one another.
Jean sees that there is scarcely any bread.
He goes off to the bakery, one minute away.
He was many years in a big hospital.
His brother doesn't want him.
Here is his home.
For many the story is the same.

Frances is here too. An assistant.
She's from England. Eighteen.
She'll be here for a year.
Mariethé is there like a gentle elder sister.
People are ushered off to work.
By 8.30 the house is quiet.

Upstairs in my room I look out over the sea.
The grey waves are white capped.
Vast breakers on the dike.
I pray the psalms and feed on the Word.

Go in the might of yours and deliver Israel
from the hands of Midian,
do I not send you?
And Gideon said to him, 'Pray Lord, how
can I deliver Israel?
Behold, my clan is the weakest in Manasseh,
and I am the least in my family.'
And the Lord said to him,
'But I will be with you.'

Such the Lord chooses.

I go down to the office for mail.
On the way I go into La Garenne.
That's where Louise died last May;
we cared for her for five months.
She taught us all a lot about death,
but even more about life.

Andrée was with her for much of that time.
I spent a little time with her; nothing deep,
but sincerely friendly.
I chat with Sarah behind her typewriter.
She needs a little time too.
I tell her about Gideon.
She smiles. 'I like that.'

Upstairs, the good finance people. Not always easy.
We are not well off. Things are tight.
'Bonjour. Bonjour. Bonjour.'
We shake hands all around. The touch is good.
If it's warm and firm, then it can speak.
I sort out an insurance problem with Christian.
I meet Elène in the corridor. She asks for time
to see me.

10.00 am. I go to the workshops for coffee.
In the joinery shop Jean-Jacques tells me
he's been here for 8 years,
and that his mother is in a home for the elderly.
He tells me every day.
He helps to make shaped supports
for Désvres china.
It's professional work.
The whole process broken down into small parts
by Jean Pierre and Didier,
the Josephs of today.
Pierrot, Jean Luc, Bernadette, Pierre,
they all have a job, they have work,

geared to their pace, to their potential.
It enables them to grow, creation continuing.
Jean-Jacques makes sure I get my coffee.
He never stops, backwards and forwards,
seeking attention, 'Look at my watch...
I'll visit my mother on Friday.'
See him prostrate before the Blessed Sacrament.
He'll be still for 30 minutes.
'Jesus is in my heart' - he really believes that.

Back to my room, like a tiny flat,
near everyone, but I'm able to be apart too.
Letters to write, a few thoughts
for the Mass tonight.
The telephone. Can I stand in for the priest at
Rinxent on Saturday evening?
I'm like a 'locum' for the
parish priests of the surrounding area.
Paul comes in.
He wants to talk about the meeting last night.
He feels he made a mess of it.
He exploded again. Relations are strained
in his house.
He longs to get it right.
We talk. Then we Pray.

Do not use harmful words in talking.
Use only helpful words, the kind that build
up and provide what is needed,
so that what you say will do good to those
who hear you...
Get rid of all bitterness, passion, and anger.
No more shouting or insults.
No more hateful feelings of any sort.
Instead, be kind and tender hearted
to one another,
and forgive one another, as God has
forgiven you in Christ.

Yes, community life is not easy.
'Come Spirit of Jesus, enable us to live
in your way.'

Tuesday. Lunch in one of the houses.
I eat somewhere different each day. That way
I can manage to keep in touch with everyone.
As I make my way through the village
I am at peace.
I meet Roger, the community 'phantom',
as he calls himself.
He's looking serious, but surely all is OK.
'Salut Roger!'
I give him a friendly pat on the back.
But all is not OK. He thumps me on the arm.
Quite hard.
I'm not sure how to handle this,

but before I make a decision he is away.
I'll have to work on this one.

At lunch I feel welcome.
The atmosphere is friendly and relaxed.
'Let's sing before we eat.'
I know this is not always the way.
Alleluia. Alleluia. Alleluia.
For the Lord, it is a pleasing noise.
Claude is beside me.
He reminds me of Popeye, with his pipe,
the way he uses his lips,
his twinkle.
I was on holiday with him for two weeks,
so we know each other well.
I can hardly understand what he says,
except when he prays, then he's really clear.

He loves going to Mass
and receiving Communion.
His mother died when he was born.
Then his aunt cared for him until
she couldn't manage any more.
He was in hospital for 39 years.
Now he gives the impression that he's lived
in the community for ever.
He's at home.
Benoît seems cheerful enough,
but he's always talking about the death
of his grandmother.
He feels she was the only one in his family
who really accepted him.
Here he's accepted by everyone.

1.45. Work begins again,
I take Bella, our dog, down to the beach,
along the promenade, past the empty
holiday homes.
Back to the house.
It takes 35 minutes.
In the afternoon I see two assistants.
One is from Poland.
We talk about prayer,
and celebrate the Sacrament of Reconciliation.
The second is from Canada.
He's thinking of staying a second year.
His parents had got things all lined up
for him at home.
'Your best chance of getting anywhere
is in engineering.'
He had said yes, but his interests
were in history and literature.
He's happy at L'Arche.
He'd like the space and the time
to think things over.

'Yes, I think I'll stay a second year.'

**Jesus asked them: 'What were you discussing
on the way?'
But they were silent; for on the way they
had discussed with one another
who was the greatest...
and Jesus said to them,
'If anyone would be first,
he must be the last of all and servant of all.'**

I glance out of the window.
A ferry from Dover passes.
The waves break over her bow.
What is it about a big ship that fascinates so?
I say the evening prayer of the Church.
I am united with the body of Christ.
United with the L'Arche communities
throughout the world,
form the West Bank to Honduras,
from Ivory Coast to Scotland.
All trying to live the mystery of the poor
in a community inspired by the Beatitudes
and the Gospel.

I need to get the big chapel ready for
the community Mass tomorrow.
As I go I meet Roger again.
'Roger, I think you have something to say to me.'
He looks at me. His face is softer now.
I know I can approach.
He moves his eyes away just a tiny bit,
slightly fearful.
I hold out my arms. So does he.
We hug. It's good. No words are necessary.
'I was really angry, wasn't I?'
He's free to talk about his feelings.

He's happy to be friends again. So am I.

It's Mass in the Oratory at 6.00 pm.
There are 7 or 8 people.
Everyone close to the altar.

**Where two or three are gathered
in my name,
there I am in the midst of them.**

Marie-Gilles is there, so
AMEN rings out loud and clear after the prayers.

At the consecration she joins in:
'... this is my body,
given for **me**.'
The difference from the words the priest says is
striking.
Marie-Gilles understands.

**I thank you, Father,
Lord of heaven and earth,
that you have hidden these things
from the learned and the clever,
and revealed them to mere children.**

Another meal. Another house.
Marcel is in a rotten mood.
He says he has pulled down his curtains.
'Come and show me.'
He takes me by the hand
and leads me to his room.
His walls are bare. It looks strange.
It's his choice.
True, there's no curtain,
but no sign of a torn one either.

I try to get him to talk about what's wrong.
I find it hard to understand.
I try to read the message.
'Shall we pray for a moment?'
'Yes.'
I ask the Spirit of peace to come,
and take away the anger, the frustration.
It's a good moment.
For a while there is peace.
Then the rotten mood comes back.
It's like that sometimes.
Night-time.
As I get back to the house people want to share
the news of the day.
'My sister is coming.'
'I cut my finger.'
'I've drawn a picture.'
'There's a new assistant coming tomorrow.'
I try to be present to each. It's not always easy.
It's good to climb the stairs to my room
and shut the door.
Even there I still hear Jeanne.
The group in the house can hardly hold her.
I know those responsible for considering
her future.
It's difficult.

People go to bed early.
Soon the house is quiet.
I read for a while.
I take a bath.

**I will lie down in peace
and sleep comes at once
for you alone, Lord, make me dwell
in safety.**

The wind has died down.

Biographical Note

Fr. David Wilson is a priest of the Diocese of Westminster. After military service and university he was ordained in 1970. For two years he worked in a parish in London, followed by two years of higher studies at the *Facultie Catholique* in Lille, France. He made a special study of the admission of people with learning difficulties to the Eucharist. On returning to England in 1974 he established a small team in the diocese with which he opened St. Joseph's Centre for pastoral work with people with learning difficulties. Fr. Wilson left the Centre in April 1987 and is now priest for a community of L'Arche in Northern France.

Note: First published in *Christian* January/February 1989, Issue number eleven. Permission of the author is gratefully acknowledged.

7 CELEBRATING THE EUCHARIST WITH PEOPLE WITH A LEARNING DIFFICULTY

Axel Liégeois

When we celebrate the Eucharist with residents who have learning difficulties in the centres of the Brothers of Charity in Flanders, there are not a few people who look on in surprise. For, indeed, we have many possibilities and opportunities to celebrate the Eucharist in a creative and authentic manner. It is in marked contrast with what we sometimes observe, when the Eucharist is reduced to an impoverished ritual, which is not understood since the people present no longer grasp the significance of the actual words and symbols. The contrast becomes sharper when we think of the period just before Vatican II. However aesthetic the Mass then was, the Latin texts, prayers and symbols had become strange and incomprehensible. Vatican II has led to significant changes for the better. In the course of this dynamic renewal, we have tried to bring the Eucharist nearer to people with a learning difficulty in order to bring them nearer to God.

It is, though, important for all the faithful to share in the gift of the Eucharist according to their capabilities. In a time of shortage of priests on the Continent, there is a growing tendency to replace the Eucharist with a prayer service. This is not bad in itself, for the liturgical tradition of the Church is much wider than just the Eucharist, and in recent decades the Eucharist was considered too often as the one and only way of gathering Christians around Christ. There are many more ways of praying and thinking on the divine without a priest presiding. Yet there is one exceptional celebration, meeting Christ under the species of bread and wine. As we do not want to prevent the faithful from meeting Christ in that very special way, we make a plea for celebrating the Eucharist in a concrete and lively manner.

How do we go about it? The key lies in the interaction between what eucharistic tradition offers us and the possibilities and life circumstances of people with a learning difficulty. We remain faithful to the essential realities of the Eucharist but we have to present them in a way adapted to the capabilities of the learning disabled and that can be recognised in their lives, their living and their lifestyle. This is a challenge. Celebrating with people who have a learning difficulty requires us to think of the meaning of the words and symbols we present to them. The celebrant will have to co-operate closely with the educators who are most closely involved. In that way the celebration of the Eucharist for people with a learning difficulty contributes to the renewal of the liturgy of the Eucharist in general. The first part of this chapter outlines the essential elements of the Eucharist: they form a harmony of symbols. The second part concretises this in a possible structure of the Eucharistic celebration.

The Eucharist as a Harmony of Symbols

The Eucharist plays an essential role in gathering the faithful who want to live in the spirit of Jesus of Nazareth, and who want to deepen this way of life. It serves as a crystallisation moment not only of the group process, but also of the faith process, the Eucharist belongs to the unutterable aspect of our experience. It has to do with walking together in life and deepening our faith. Celebrating the Eucharist is an all-embracing experience.

The meeting of believers is, of course, a meeting of people. We communicate with others via human, interpretable signs. The Eucharist is made up of symbols that refer to a reality beyond the senses. It is as a wedding ring which represents more than 5 grams of gold made into a ring. In the Eucharist these symbols point to God and his People via the life of Jesus. As of old, symbols are used to express these realities. Here they follow.

A gathering of like-minded people

The Eucharist convenes Christians and those who want to become Christians. It is a ritual through which we commit ourselves - not just one of the many rituals. Neither is it a private devotion, nor a cosy club meeting. The Eucharist is essentially a community event. Its celebration is the result of a development within the community. We have reason to celebrate and our interrelationship invites it. Solidarity among humans is the earth in which the Eucharist is rooted: we recognise one another as pilgrims on the way of Jesus of Nazareth, and we affirm and encourage one another.

Life confronted with the Bible

The extraordinary value of the Eucharist is found in the hard manner of confrontation between one's own life (realisation and faults, dreams and disappointments, expectations and illusions) and the dream, the expectation, the vision of man and his world based on the Bible. This confrontation calls for an evaluation of our own situation in the light of the other reality which the Biblical tradition offers. It affirms us in every step forward we make on the way.

This confrontation opens perspectives on the actual steps we have to take in order to concretise our vision. It invites us to foster attitudes like forgiving, trust, and seeking to do right, which we do not always uphold naturally. We are assisted by the encouraging example of the community of like-minded people to realise these attitudes in our own life.

A Bible reading is essential to the realisation of the set ideals. The choice of the reading matters. Sometimes we take non-biblical texts that happen to be more pertinent to the experience of disabled people. If, however, such a text is used, we advise taking an additional text from the Old or New Testament. For we have gathered to confront our lives with the story of the People of Israel and of Jesus of Nazareth. When it comes to explaining that text we can use other stories, texts, and songs.

Moreover, it is desirable that the text of the Sunday Readings is understood. Sometime we opt for a theme; but experience has taught us that we are mostly satisfied with a limited range of texts. It can make sense to confront ourselves with a text we have not chosen, but which belongs to the essence of the Bible. It may happen that we do not readily see the meaning of the message for our time, but the confrontation will always deliver something positive if we go sufficiently deeply into it. It's better not to offer an abundance of readings, for it makes the understanding of the whole rather difficult. There is no need to tell all in one celebration. One aspect of an idea per celebration is more than enough, not only because there are other celebrations to follow but because the celebration is not just an intellectual thing. Living the faith is at least equally important.

Two ritual items have found their place here: the Penitential Rite and the Profession of Faith. Gradually they acquired their regular place. The question is whether they have to be there in every Eucharistic celebration. Another question is their location in the sequence of the celebrations. The custom of having the penitential rite very early in the celebration may have a negative impact. Why should we start with referring to our sinfulness? The African liturgy puts the penitential rite after the readings and homily: having listened to the Word, we are ready to forsake our shortcomings to the Message, according to each person's potential, and to confess our faith in Him whom we proclaim.

Although each of these elements are meaningful, they do not seem to be necessary to every celebration. Their occasional use will avoid routine and may serve to focus our particular attention on them.

Table-companionship

We come together at a table. The story of Jesus offers us this table-community as a life-community. The Eucharist is not a business lunch but a meal among friends, in all intimacy. It concerns people who are committed to solidarity with the Gospel options. What we heard in words is 'consumed' in a shared meal. It is an eminent symbol of the celebration of life, the expression and living of solidarity. It tells us who we are and who we want to be.

The breaking of the bread

The sign of breaking bread is a gesture of life. It supposes a fundamental choice of openness and solidarity with others, small and great. It is in contrast with piling up and hoarding for oneself. It is an expression of our will to overcome all obstacles of a personal and cultural nature, in our going out to and sharing with others. It is not non-committal: the one who acts this symbol wants to move away from the ego in order to allow the other one in, to welcome the weak and the poor, by preference.

Sharing the cup

Besides the breaking of bread, a symbol of daily life, the cup of the Covenant is shared as well. This is an expression of our faith that the reality of life, however hard its circumstances may be, is not the final thing for humanity. For every situation, however painful, there is the outlook to a dream and a solidarity that reaches beyond the visible things. What is not today may be tomorrow. This dream is gradually realised as we carry it through life.

Signs of bread and wine are archetypes which the history of mankind has handed down to us. They are not easily substituted by other signs or symbols. Chips and Coke cannot take their place. Meanwhile, we have the task of finding ways and means to make these symbols as familiar as possible.

Praying to God

We find all this in the story of Jesus of Nazareth, in the memory of His life, death and resurrection. Here we address explicitly the God whom Jesus called His Father. We express our faith in the fact that God is approachable, that He hears and understands us, that He wants to live among us, His people, so that we can communicate with Him.

The celebrant should be able to express in the prayers that are said aloud what concerns the community. Tradition foresees some prayers: the Opening Prayer and the Prayer after Communion. At the offertory (the preparation of the altar and the gifts) a prayer can be introduced, although it is not always desirable as there is a liturgical prayer of offering.

There are another two important prayers: the Intercessions and the Eucharistic Prayer. The liturgy of the Word gave the community the opportunity to take part in the prayers by means of the Intercessions. They invite the whole community to unite with the prayers said in common, the petitions, the needs, and the concerns of the members of the community. When the liturgy of the Word is followed by the liturgy of the Eucharist, the Intercessions might be said just after the consecration, and they are rounded off by saying together the Our Father. Before closing off the celebration the intentions of the community can be mentioned again, but during the liturgy of the Eucharist they can take place during the Eucharistic Prayer.

The Eucharistic Prayer is, traditionally, the central part of the liturgy of the Eucharist. Here the essence of the Eucharist (a Greek word meaning thanksgiving) is announced. The Eucharistic Prayer consists of three parts. First of all, there is the prayer of thanksgiving, the Preface. We give thanks for all the good gifts granted us, for God's love, for knowing Jesus. Together with the celebrant the people present can express their thanks. This is obvious in celebrations by people who are on familiar terms; otherwise the celebrant gives thanks on behalf of the community he represents.

Thereafter, we give thanks for Jesus of Nazareth. We commemorate His life, death and resurrection; the Last Supper is retold and actualised.

Finally, we pray for God's Spirit, for the Church, mankind, the deceased and for our own community. During a celebration by an intimate group, the prayers of the members of the community can be expressed. At larger gatherings the celebrant will offer the prayers.

Personal prayer remains, of course, important for everyone who attends. Therefore, the Church has foreseen moments of silence during the Eucharistic celebration so that each member can unite with the prayers of the community.

A Possible Structure of the Eucharistic Celebration

The harmony of symbols which the Eucharist is, can be concretised in the following structure. From olden times the Eucharist has been divided into two main parts, each one with its own character: the liturgy of the Word and the liturgy of the Eucharist. In the first mentioned part, the following signs come to the fore: the meeting of like-minded people; the confrontation between life and Bible; and praying to God. According to tradition, this first part has always been accessible to all, even to non-Christians. All those who want to get to know Christianity can still share in this part of the celebration. It is the initiation moment of every celebration. The liturgy of the Word leaves a lot of scope for creativity. It can be celebrated without a priest presiding over it or being too much involved with its preparation so that this first part of the Eucharist can be well prepared by the more intimate group of believers.

The second part, the liturgy of the Eucharist, has other typical signs: sharing the table, breaking the bread, sharing the cup and praying to God. It is the supreme moment of celebrating in deep union with God and the believers. Therefore, non-baptised people were not allowed to attend in former times. The custom of leaving church after the offering during funeral Masses goes back to those times. The intimacy of this part of the celebration requires a special attitude and attention. Christians are put here in the presence of God through words and signs. In this spiritual event people experience God's presence in prayer, in the breaking of the bread, and sharing the same vision on future blessedness.

As to the place in which to celebrate the Eucharist, we prefer a chapel or church. The place of prayer should be so arranged that it is conducive to communication, participation, and community among the participants. We can indicate the transition from the liturgy of the Word to the liturgy of the Eucharist by moving the action from one area to another. The readings are done from a lectern put nearer the entrance to the chapel. Thereafter, the faithful can move deeper into the chapel to the altar and form a circle around it to celebrate the liturgy of the Eucharist. In the old liturgies this spatial distinction was generally upheld.

Before describing a possible structure of the Eucharistic Celebration, we want to stress that the Eucharist is the focal point of living the faith and of human solidarity as well. The celebration is embedded in the life of the believing community, and starts with the preliminary celebration or preparation while ending in an after-celebration.

The video made during a Eucharistic Celebration in Our Lady of the Dunes, Koksijde in Belgium, on 30 June 1996, can be referred to for a true image of this holy event.

Preparation

The preparation for the celebration is part of the life of the community of believers. The community prepares the celebration by means of rehearsing hymns, and by learning the instructions for a smooth participation in the celebration. People are welcomed on entering the church. We are going to celebrate a great feast, the feast of Jesus. The officiating priest may put on a festive robe made by the children.

The Introductory Rites

The celebration begins with the greeting. This community has gathered to celebrate, and we want to know who takes part. The names of the people present, and their age groups may be mentioned. The reasons for coming together and the principal themes can be announced.

Apart from ourselves, there is Somebody present among the people gathered. Therefore, we greet one another in His name: we make the Sign of the Cross. If the Sign of the Cross is already difficult for some residents, we may substitute a simplified sign of solidarity. Instead of referring to the three divine Persons, "*In the Name of the Father, the Son and the Holy Spirit*", we can refer to Jesus only, "*We know Jesus; we love Jesus; for ever.*" Meanwhile the same Sign of the Cross is made in the ordinary way of bringing the hand to the forehead (knowing), to the heart (loving) and from the left to the right shoulder (forever).

Then comes the Opening Prayer. It is to be said, not read, as an address to God. Thereafter we spend some moments in silence. We take fire from the vigil lamp and enkindle the Pascal candle to help us realise that we are in God's presence and are allowed to talk to him.

The Penitential Rite may follow now, although we prefer it to be put it after the Readings.

Everyone is welcomed to the celebration. Names are mentioned... people meet to rejoice together. All those who attend, or even those left at home, make the Sign of the Cross together. Candles are lit at a celebration. 'Quarrelling', 'pestering', 'self-centredness' can only spoil the right atmosphere, for then the light goes out. From the Pascal candle, symbolising Jesus, we take light to light our candles. After a prayer for forgiveness we express our thankfulness through a hymn of praise, the Gloria, and by burning incense.

We spend some moments in silence before addressing God in the Opening Prayer.

The Liturgy of the Word

Now we confront our lives with the Bible. In order to impress the authority of the Bible on the participants, we can make use of a voluminous book. The text can be read or narrated. Listening to the Readings can be supported by audio-visual aids, for it is advisable to help the understanding of learning disabled listeners by calling in several senses. The text can be illustrated by means of slides or transparencies with drawings or pictures. Residents might impersonate characters of the Bible story in a scene or tableau.

After the reading, several elements of the celebration may follow: the homily, The Penitential Rite and the Profession of Faith. If the residents' understanding is up to it, the Bible story can be explained in a simple homily. Confessing our shortcomings in the Penitential Rite or asking forgiveness may result from the confrontation with the Bible. All sorts of visual aids can be used here. Finally, the proclamation of the Message may be followed by a Profession of Faith. It is desirable to make use of only one of these three elements.

A hymn introduces us to the theme of the Reading, for example 'Do not be afraid,' Mathew 6: 25. Thereafter we listen to the words taken from the Book of Jesus (a big Bible brought forward in the company of light-bearers). The hymn, used as a homily, should make the Gospel message more explicit to us in our circumstances.

Our faith is being challenged. At the end of each article of the Profession of Faith, we could affirm it by lighting a candle from the Pascal candle.

Transition

After the confrontation with the Word, a pause is made to prepare for the intense moment of prayer of the liturgy of the Eucharist. This transition can be expressed by our moving to the altar to form a circle around it.

The table (altar) can be brought to that spot and can be prepared. Only the essential items are put on the table: a tablecloth, a dish with bread, a cup, a jug or bottle of wine, sober decorations, flowers and a pair of candles. The less verbally developed residents can lend a hand at this moment.

The officiating priest invites the people to set the table, for Jesus wants to come among us through these signs.

The Liturgy of the Eucharist

The Eucharistic Prayer is the supreme moment for thanksgiving, commemorating the Last Supper of Jesus, and allowing us to make our petitions. As a thanksgiving we can have people bringing flowers or objects that give the residents pleasure to the altar, show them and thank God for them. The Lord's supper is narrated. Breaking the Bread and sharing the Cup must be clearly shown. The distribution of bread and wine is done in different directions. While making our petitions we can have candles brought forward, or have them already put on candlesticks with the names of those for whom we pray.

Then follows the Lord's Prayer. Together we say the prayer Jesus taught us. We may say it while making body movements or depicting it. We can sing it to a contemporary tune. As we cannot sit at table with people unless we are at peace with them, we express our willingness for this peace by the sign of peace, shaking hands or hugging, or handing over a drawing made beforehand.

At Communion, we may have some residents helping with the breaking of the bread to help to emphasise the sharing. Receiving is adapted to the potential of the residents. They may receive under the two species, for example by dipping the 'Bread' in the 'Wine'.

The Eucharistic Prayer has three parts:

- The first part is sung, supported by gestures to facilitate the understanding. Flowers are brought time and again.

- After the Preface, the story of Jesus' Last Supper is narrated (consecration).

- Thereafter we pray to God for many people.

A burning candle is brought forward every time we make a petition for those like us, for the sick, for the rejoicing, for the poor, or for the deceased. When the altar is fully prepared, we sing the Our Father, Jesus' own prayer.

The sign of peace: a friendly invitation to join the meal.
The breaking of the Bread: sharing the Bread is a sign of genuine solidarity with others.
The communion.

Concluding Rite

At the end of the celebration the theme may be repeated. In the Prayer after Communion we express our thanks again. At the Blessing, we wish one another good luck in God's name. We may make the Sign of the Cross as we did at the start of the celebration.
We sing and dance for joy because Jesus is among us. Thereafter we spend some moments in silence before the Prayer after Communion.

After-celebration

After the eucharistic celebration we may remain together for some time to meet and talk a little longer. On special occasions we might extend the celebration into the festivities outside the church.

The feast is continued, everybody is invited to share in the festive cake.

CONCLUSION

It seems of the utmost importance that the Eucharist is not limited to the liturgy of the Word, however important it may be. The liturgy of the Word allows for great creativity and the input of many to prepare for the confrontation with the Bible. Moreover, Christianity offers the gift of Christ's presence in the symbols of bread and wine. Taking part in the liturgy of the Eucharist is an eminent source of inspiration for the lives of the faithful. Celebrating the Eucharist with God himself in union with Jesus of Nazareth is a mighty step forward in relationship building with God, our Father. In that way the Eucharist is of the essence of Christianity. It would be a tragedy if this supreme gift of God would not reach our special people.

Biographical Note
Alel Liégeois studied moral theology at Louvain Catholic University in Belgium, where he obtained the degree of Doctor in Sacred Theology. Since 1989, he is a Staff member of the Pastoral and Ethical Service in the Provincial House of the Brothers of Charity in Belgium. He is responsible for the co-ordination of pastoral care and ethical reflection in Mental Health Care and the Care for People with an Intellectual Disability. He presides over the Pastoral Care Committee in the Care for People with an Intellectual Disability. Recently, he has published a book in Dutch on ethics in mental health care, *Begrensde vrijheid: Etjiek in de geestelijke gezondheidszorg* (Limited Freedom: Ethics in Mental Health Care), 1997, Kapellen, Belguim: Pelckmans.

Acknowledgment
The author wishes to express his thanks and appreciation to the members of the Pastoral Care Committee in the Care for People with an intellectual disability at the Brothers of Charity in Belgium namely, Jan De Leener and

Rudy Dubois (Bellingen, Huize Terloo), Chris Nollet (Brecht, O.C. Clara Fey), Lieven De Vulder (Brussel, K.I. voor Doven en Blinden), Paul Blanckaert (Gent, O.C. Sint-Jozef), Guido Moons and Fons Van Wielendaele (Gent, O.C. Sint-Juliaan), Axel Liégeois (Gent, Provincialaat), Filip D'Hooghe and Jef Goethals (Gentbrugge, O.C. Sint-Gregorius), Christiane De Prez and Luc Lemmens (Gijzenzele, Nursingtehuis De Beweging), Bart Moens (Leuven, Het Roerhuis), Jan Decoene (Lummen, O.C. Sint-Ferdinand), Jean-Marie Catry and Toon Vandeputte (Roeselare, O.C. Sint-Idesbald)

The video of the Celebration in Our Lady of The Dunes on 30 June 1996 is available from Lisieux Hall.

8 ESTABLISHING A PASTORAL CARE SERVICE IN GALWAY

Claude Madec

This chapter reports on a pilot period of five years during which a pastoral programme has gradually developed and found its place at the heart of a service for people with learning disabilities in County Galway and Roscommon, Ireland.

'Pastoral care? Is it something new?'
'What is this about?'
'Are you a priest or a brother?'
'I am not religious...'
'I am not available after working hours...'
'This is something really important for the lads, I have been saying it for so long... Our people should have access to the sacraments and have opportunities to go on a pilgrimage like anybody else.'
'We have no budget for this...'
'It is about prayer and mass isn't it?'
'The local priest calls in from time to time.'
'But, what will you be doing exactly?'

These are some of the comments I was greeted with five years ago. In recalling some of these questions and comments gathered here and there in the early days of my appointment, I have come to realise what a long way we have travelled since January 1993, but I am also aware that some of these questions raise important issues which need acknowledgement and clarification.

This chapter offers some reflection on the nature and place of the pastoral dimension as it has evolved in the Brothers of Charity Galway Services, and includes its history, its brief as it has developed to date, some reflections on the approach and philosophy which have played an important role in shaping the venture, and a comprehensive illustration of the contribution this programme has made to the lives of our services, its people and their communities. The last section looks at some of the challenges that lie in front of us and makes recommendations for the future development of this already thriving pastoral programme.

Appointment of a Pastoral Co-ordinator

Following the report and recommendations of a Pastoral Care Commission which was set up in the Brothers of Charity Services in 1989, the Brother Provincial appointed me as Pastoral Co-ordinator to see to the re-kindling and development of a pastoral dimension in the services. I took up employment as Pastoral co-ordinator in January 1993, having completed a graduate programme in Pastoral Studies at La Salle University in Philadelphia. This was an appointment with a national brief for a period of five years.

This was an exciting departure from the point of view of the vision, challenges and the potential it carried; but it was also a daunting task for which there were no formal supportive networks or structures yet in place. My involvement at a national level was not to last. The lack of supportive networks and distances made an effective national contribution far too difficult. By late spring 1995 with the Provincial's agreement, it was decided that my field would be limited to Counties Galway and Roscommon.

"Something Old and Something New..."

Isn't it surprising in many ways that this "pastoral dimension" should have been considered as "something new" when the original inspiration and vision of the organisation is driven by Gospel values which are espoused by the Brothers of Charity and which are essentially pastoral. These values and the underlying principles of our services as articulated in several internal publications of the Services such as *Creating Service Communities where Relationship is a Core Value* (1992) and *Structure in the Brothers of Charity* (1995), point towards a holistic approach to service provision. Our services are indeed the legacy of the founder, Peter Triest, and the communities we seek to build with people with a learning disability are inspired by a vision which sees a pastoral response as the call of the Gospel, a call that claims dignity and life to the full for all, regardless of who we are, with or without disability, carers and cared for.

Pastoral care has often been defined as, 'any human care whose motivation and/or delivery is theological and/or spiritual.' This definition which is inclusive of many religious and philosophical traditions helps us realise the width and breadth of pastoral care, its many facets and the many contexts from which it might develop.

The programme we are concerned with, and to which we refer as The Brothers of Charity *Pastoral Programme*, for the lack of a better term, plays a valuable role in this Service which takes a holistic approach to service provision. Like the many other facets of our Service it contributes in its own way and in an integrated manner to enhance quality of life for those it reaches, pushing open for them and with them doors that lead to life in all its fullness.

"That they may have life and life to the full"

In the above context the aim of the pastoral programme has been to offer support within the services in the area of human and spiritual development at a personal and community level, thereby fulfilling an important dimension of the Brothers of Charity ethos. In so doing the programme develops a wide range of opportunities which contributes to enhance quality of life for service-users and their communities.

This programme is guided by the principles of integration and advocacy that are already identified as core policies of service provision; it is motivated by the desire to uphold the dignity of the people it reaches, the desire to promote personal growth and meaningful relationships; and the desire to respect and support the right of the person to a spiritual life and the freedom of each one to practise and grow in his or her Faith tradition.

This vision and the means of its implementation are reflected in the following brief which is shaped by the original Service's vision to re-kindle and develop the pastoral dimension in the services with attention given to the needs and suggestions of service users, members of staff and their respective communities.

The principal function of the pastoral care programme, is to offer support within the services in the area of human and spiritual development, at a personal and community level. The objectives are as follows.

Promote awareness and understanding of Pastoral care

To promote awareness it is necessary to create spaces where opportunities are given to discover, sense, and understand the nature of pastoral care at personal, community, local and regional level. This includes hosting workshops, celebrations and other appropriate events.

Promoting awareness involves networking and disseminating information.

It is necessary to encourage staff to acknowledge the pastoral needs of those whom they assist and invite them to actively support what is offered by the programme.

Nurture spiritual development

The Services acknowledge the importance of the spiritual dimension in people's life and the rights and wishes of service users (and of their families) to practise and grow in their faith. To this end the pastoral programme is engaged to:
1.   co-ordinate various styles of retreats and times of renewal made available to service users, staff and families;
2.   co-ordinate and facilitate times of prayer and reflection in consultation with centres or other programmes within the service;
3.   co-ordinate inter-centre seasonal liturgical celebrations;
4.   organise pilgrimages;
5.   research and design appropriate 'catechetical' and liturgical material;
6.   offer centres and programmes support and facilitation in

preparing liturgies, celebrations of the sacraments, and catecheses; and

7.   provide support to local organisations such as Faith and Light which also seek to nurture the spiritual needs of people with an intellectual disability and their families.

Nurture personal development

The role of the pastoral care programme here is to identify and prioritise needs and suggestions with service-users and/or members of staff and to offer to co-ordinate activities, courses and projects enhancing quality of life and fostering personal development. These may include (and have included):

Art, Music, and Drama;
Support groups;
Weekend and midweek-breaks; and
Leisure based activities.

The programmes support inter-centre events which help people keep in touch with each other and with their families and communities. The programme contributes to staff support and renewal.

Nurture community development

To this end, the pastoral care programme is engaged to initiate and be of support in the planning and organisation of various events where a greater sense of identity and togetherness can be experienced at local or regional levels. This may include various gatherings and celebrations around a specific focus such as a retreat in Esker, a Harvest festival, the Vanier retreat, the Esker Fest and so on.

The programmes attempt to create spaces where people with an intellectual disability and staff can be renewed in their relationships.

We try to look at ways of developing contacts between service users and non-front line personnel.

We focus on supporting community awareness projects.

Contribute to nurturing of ethos in the Brothers of Charity Services

The pastoral care Programme has a role in initiating and being of support in the planning and organisation of various events or projects where the understanding of our vision can be explored, deepened, renewed and celebrated; and in contributing to aspects of evaluation of our Services.

Develop a supportive and structured network

The pastoral care programme plays a role in supporting and affirming members of staff and service-users who show interest in and commitment to the development of a pastoral dimension in their respective centres; co-ordinating local and regional pastoral teams; recruiting and motivating volunteers for specific projects; liaising with the appropriate support services; and maintaining and developing links with other organisations.

Maintain and develop pastoral resources

At a practical level the pastoral care programme tries to keep up to date with current publications; maintain and develop a pastoral library; maintain and develop liturgical and catechetical multi-sensory material; and manage the pastoral budget.

Evaluate the programme

The direction of the pastoral care programme is reviewed annually and on an ongoing basis in order to evaluate projects, and ask service-users and members of staff for both formal or informal feedback. The measure is qualitative rather than quantitative.

The programme gathers the findings of evaluations and prioritises the new needs, relaying them to the appropriate channels, pastoral teams and centres.

THE MUSTARD SEED

Over the past five years, and especially in the early days, I have met with people who had mixed feelings about the pastoral programme. They had in mind the more narrow religious perspective of such a programme, or considered it as '*icing on the cake*' and therefore far from being a priority at any level it was sometimes even feared as being another demand on already busy work schedules.

When one has experienced disillusionment with churches or services; the hardship of long working days; a sense of not feeling heard or valued; shortages of funding for programmes; and the lack of spaces for making sense of what we live, it is hardly surprising one wouldn't have questions about the 'new pastoral venture'.

I spent a lot of time in the first few months meeting and listening to people's questions and hearing of their hopes for this 'new venture' and discovering the intricate fabric of our services. Relationships of trust had to be established, in a sense I had to become part of the Brothers of Charity community.

The initial daunting face of a service soon filled with many warm and welcoming faces. I became part of their life and they became part of mine trusting we each had something in store for the other. I am deeply grateful to those among our staff who gave me their support and encouragement and still do; they believed with me in the potential of this pastoral programme.

I saw this human face first in the service-users themselves who welcomed me so warmly and showed so much enthusiasm in whatever they were offered, and this convinced me as well as others, that there was a future for the venture. Their openness and their capacity to judge what enriches the quality of their lives, their affirming gestures and unequivocal suggestions have given this pastoral programme the direction it has taken. They share in an important way in the successful re-kindling of this pastoral dimension.

The pace was gentle. That of the mustard seed: the seed is sown in the ground and slowly it becomes a bush in which the birds of the air come to build their nest.

It takes time and patience for anything to grow and during this slow process, many people closely associated with the development of this pastoral dimension have experienced frustration and at times discouragement, but with this comes also the warm harvest days where struggles find meaning and are transcended in the togetherness of our celebrations.

The pastoral programme was taking its first steps at a time when there was much soul-searching in the services. The word 'ethos' was on so many lips! Shortly after I commenced, *Structures in the Brothers of Charity Services* was published.

I believe that although the pastoral programme was developing independently of this process, the changing climate of the time served it well. There was now a greater awareness of the programme and more openness towards what it was offering in initiating new activities and creating spaces where one could experience and recognise much of what was said about relationship, community, belonging, celebration, and quality of life.

Come and see...

An important aspect of my brief has been to promote awareness and understanding of Pastoral Care. There is never only one way of introducing a new departure but the choice of method is crucial. The method must take into account the context in which it must operate, the people to be reached, and it must reflect closely the ethos that moves the project.

Ours has been a 'come and see...' approach. It is a humble but powerful model. Much energy went into networking, building a relationship of trust and calling people forth to places where they would not feel threatened and could experience for themselves the essence of what this pastoral programme is about.

The choice of this approach, which was primarily experiential, was aimed at reaching two populations; people with an intellectual disability, and members of staff, and the task was to bring them together as one community.

Life in our services would be very impoverished if there were no efforts put into building relationships and community. The building and nourishing of relationships and community has been one important focus of the pastoral programme and all that has been offered starts from the premise that regardless of disabilities we share in the same humanity each and every one of us with our gifts and our needs. Our needs to be recognised and valued for who we are, and to be loved, our needs to be understood when it hurts inside, our need for relationship and to give, as much as to receive, our need of knowing that we can make a difference in somebody's life. Our gift of warmth and welcome, our gifts of openness and forgiveness, our gifts of sharing and listening and our gifts of affirmation and of healing. It is when we become conscious of this interconnectedness that relationships can truly become life-giving for all.

In order that our gifts meet our needs, I saw it as my job to create spaces where members of staff could open up to new experiences, or re-discover for themselves the richness of the vision with which they set out in their choice of working with people with an intellectual disability. For service users, these spaces have provided them with rich opportunities of personal affirmation.

The space of pastoral care is that of awareness and discovery, of shared journeys we seek to articulate and celebrate. I am not saying for a moment that this consciousness is absent from the busy pace of life in our centres, but it needs nurturing; this is too important to be left unaddressed, for it is in this consciousness that we can be a service with a strong identity. I am happy that the pastoral programme has made a contribution in areas by facilitating some of these moments of renewal of which it is not the exclusive conveyor.

This pastoral space involves a wide range of new experiences through activities such as drama, music and various other art forms where you are invited to let Life - your capacity to become you more fully - take you by surprise and push you to new heights to experience something never felt before and which widens your horizon, renews your self-esteem and gives you new insights.

Evaluation and self advocacy

The pastoral programme is committed to seeing that what is offered is not left to be a flash in the pan. One key element to this process is that in addition to the casual feedback they give the participants, service-users and staff are also asked to evaluate more formally what is offered, be it a retreat, liturgy, a pastoral series of sessions, a festival or other event.

The evaluation formats vary according to the target group, the object of the research, and its timing; overall a special effort goes into making this exercise user-friendly and inclusive, making sure all can make their voice heard. It may happen through filling in evaluation forms, through group work, through an open forum, and wider surveys. The comments and suggestions are then gathered and taken on board for future pastoral planning giving the 'evaluators' opportunities of claiming a greater ownership of the programme. This programme takes pride in the wide range of options and experiences it offers, providing thereby a rich ground for personal development and greater self awareness from which self advocacy skills can naturally develop. Indeed the preferences, suggestions, and needs voiced by service-users have played a strong role in defining the direction this pastoral programme has taken to date.

Team building

Networking and team building are essential for the development of such a programme. The last two to three years have seen a large increase in the number and range of activities facilitated by this department, and it is obvious that this would not have happened without the support received from colleagues from the four corners of both Galway and Roscommon.

In County Roscommon, a pastoral team was formed following one of the 'Pastoral care in context' workshops. This active group meets regularly to co-ordinate, prepare, and host various events throughout the year. The evaluation survey it ran in late 1996, paved the way for a rich series of pastoral events for 1997. The team receives much support from the Director of Services.

Although the Galway services haven't yet got a regional pastoral team as such, members of staff and service users representing our community programmes for adults do meet to plan and prepare for inter-centre events. There is little that could have happened without their ongoing dedication to the pastoral venture and their advocacy on behalf of service-users. While for some people the task hasn't been an easy one because the support they needed was not consistently available at their centres, for others the amount of scope and initiatives left to them made for a more pleasant experience and a greater participation of service-users in events hosted by the programme. I trust that a formal taking-on-board of the pastoral programme by the services and the formulation of a pastoral care policy should address these difficulties.

Volunteering

As we are all too aware, volunteering is greatly underdeveloped in our services. This unfortunately also applies to the pastoral programme. Nonetheless, some very positive experiences, such as the involvement of volunteers on the *Ar Scáth a Chéile* retreats, art sessions, evenings of reflection, and the *CÁIRDE* programme summarised here below, have shown the potential of volunteering as a support to this programme and to those who benefit from it.

The CÁIRDE volunteer pilot project

The goal of this project was to invite two young men or women to work in our services for a year as a support to volunteers to further the development of the pastoral dimension in our services. It was envisaged that this pilot project would contribute towards answering the great need for the support and facilitation which will enable people with an intellectual disability to engage more fully in leisure activities, and have a greater choice of options available to them and to participate more meaningfully in activities fostering personal and community development.

The *CÁIRDE* volunteers would also provide support to the programme co-ordinator in organising and running projects which might not always be directly connected with their focus community.

In view of the constantly growing number and diversity of activities which are requested and offered, practical help is often needed for a more effective preparation and facilitation of events. *CÁIRDE* provides much assistance in this regard.

The pilot project embraced the principles of self advocacy and offered a context within which the Service Users had many opportunities of input in the planning of activities and overall shaping of the programme. The name of the project, *CÁIRDE* (Irish for 'friends') illustrates well the spirit in which the volunteers were invited to come on board. The provision of activities was not seen as the sole focus of *CÁIRDE,* but with it the building of a relationship of trust, friendship and companionship, which could pave a way for growth for all parties, with an appreciation of each other and the recognition of the richness of this experience for one's life and its impact on our services for adults in local communities.

One of our two volunteers had to leave the programme in the early days, the other, Heather Fox, completed her year and became fully part of the Service in which she worked. She was very enthusiastic from the start, and soon was able to show initiative and take responsibilities. She was determined and gave all she had to make this project a success.

This *CÁIRDE* Pilot Project, which is evaluated in a separate report, proved to be a great success as it made a significant difference in the lives of the people it touched.

Developing and maintaining pastoral resources

Over the past five years, I have gradually built up a very valuable pastoral resource which includes tapes, publications, liturgical material, art, drama, multi-sensory materials, and percussion instruments. These can be borrowed free of charge. The managing of this resource is not an easy task; the occasional help I have received form volunteers to keep it in shape has been appreciated.

GATHERINGS

This section is a comprehensive illustration of what has been offered by this programme. As I have outlined already, personal spiritual and community development have been identified as important aspects to be addressed. Although I have presented them separately, it is clear that the divisions are functional rather than intrinsic. In the various projects I have tried to honour all of these dimensions simultaneously.

Celebration and Liturgy -
Re-discovering gestures that speak, and words that touch

Celebration, the more ritualised aspect of pastoral care holds an important place in the programme. In a society or service which seem to take on a more secular visage there is a danger of excluding the ritualised expressions of our lives because we fear a religious label. We need, I think, to remember that rituals and celebrations are not the property of religion alone but of men and women who in society try to articulate what they live in relation to their own inner life. The word ritual evokes many rich images but overall, ritual can be defined as, *'the dramatic form through which people and community make tangible in symbols, gesture, word and song what they have come to believe is the hidden meaning of their experience in relationship with others.'* So indeed we will find at the heart of our celebrations a very spiritual and inspiring dimension. The failure in finding there the uplifting gestures, words and emotions that help us transcend the routines of our daily lives, could only reveal barrenness or at best the lack of a deep understanding of what this is about.

Celebrations deserve adequate time for preparation. It is a crucial time when we struggle to unfold the holiness of all that is profane to reveal the sacred qualities of secular life. Ritualisation doesn't just happen. It must come as the fruit of a genuine reflection on our lives and a search for meaning - or else there is a risk of losing its authenticity and failing to inspire.

The pastoral programme has put much effort into giving people the means of developing beautiful rituals and liturgies which become genuine places of nourishment for both individuals and communities, and a genuine celebration of the ethos that moves us. Liturgies can only be life giving when they rise from, and flow back into, the life which we share.

These rituals, whether Christian or not, must not be seen as superfluous but as a profound means of bringing us closer together, client, nurse or psychologist, parent or social worker, caterer or secretary, to transcend the day-to-day routine, leaving behind the professional and carer/cared-for divides to consciously acknowledge our interconnectedness and be re-energised. These moments I believe are absolutely necessary for our services in order to claim and celebrate the rich philosophy it upholds.

We need to find or re-discover gestures that speak, and words that touch to celebrate our lives. In acknowledging the importance of the spiritual dimension in people's lives, and the right and wishes of service users (and of their families) to practise their faith, this programme supports and co-ordinates a wide range of events and activities which promote spiritual and faith development.

As in the case of celebration, spiritual development does not happen in a vacuum. It is not removed or ethereal, but well anchored in our relationship to the world around us and shaped by the faith of the community to which we belong. This programme has long rejected the idea of 'special liturgies' or 'special catechesis' for 'special people'. The fact is that liturgy is liturgy, and catechesis is catechesis, and all partakers, regardless of disabilities are invited to share at the table of God's covenant.

In order to make these liturgies and catechetical sessions meaningful experiences for both staff and service-users, this programme encourages the various groups or communities which ask for support to opt for a 'symbolic approach'. In general much care is given to the creation of safe spaces where one can experience a sense of belonging and engage in catecheses, and rituals, and where attention is given to connect life experiences and worship. We look back, we recall events and feelings through using our senses, the symbols we handle bring us to moments of insight that help us situate ourselves, to search, and to celebrate God with us.

The greater the disability, the greater the challenge. This can be true but is not necessarily so. Nothing is ever impossible. Let us remember that both our cognitive and intuitive capacities can play an important role in faith development. People with an intellectual disability rely more on their intuitive capacity for their Faith journey. We must always consider people first, we consider their way of relating and engaging, then we look at the focus of the celebration and find the appropriate inclusive gestures and words that will communicate what is intended. Too often the, 'Aren't they little angels', or 'They have no sins' has been an excuse to cover our inadequacies and leave it all to 'God's grace' forgetting that the Christian model of revelation which is incarnational is addressed to all and especially to those who are most alienated. I have met so many parents who have been deeply hurt by the lack of sensitivity of clergy. But I have also seen how in places like St. Michael's at the John Paul Centre in Galway, people with a profound disability and their carers have lived together very powerful moments of prayer.

The pastoral programme has offered support and nourishment on this journey by facilitating the following.

Workshops - "Community and Liturgy"

This first workshop held in Kinvar, was offered as a forum for 25 people involved in liturgy in our services. As the title of the course indicates, the emphasis was put on rooting liturgy in contexts and in community. It was a great opportunity for getting to know each other better, finding support from colleagues and for the organiser of the workshop to assess needs. The format of this workshop met with much enthusiasm.

Religious education, prayer and celebration with people with a learning disability

The aim of this two-day workshop was to give people who work in child development centres, special schools and adult services an opportunity to reflect on the place of religious education, prayer, and celebration in the lives of people with an intellectual disability. We looked at the importance of responding to the senses in the preparation of prayer spaces, the use of symbols and the planning of celebrations taking into account the rhythms of the seasons and the events in our lives as shaped by the community and the culture to which we belong.

Retreats and times of renewal

These days which are built around a theme, included drama, story-telling, outside activities, banner making, times of prayer and reflection - all of this with plenty of room for good humour and togetherness: '*All were given the opportunity to participate fully in the day's events whether it was drama, where we had such fun and a feeling of euphoria, to the relaxation of a simple lunch which we enjoyed together;' 'The beautiful liturgy that closes the day in Esker is a rich moment where we experience a great sense of belonging;' and 'The Atmosphere in Esker each year leaves us with a great feeling of peace and well-being.'*

Both St. Clare's and St. Kevin's programme at the John Paul Centre have had similar experiences in Esker. The following feedback points to witness to very worthwhile days out. 'We needed so much to get together as a group.' 'We would have loved to stay there for much longer. It was such a relaxing atmosphere.' 'It was so much fun, we discovered each other in new ways...' 'It was a great day for letting down our hair...' 'There was plenty of variety for all service-users and member of staff... We all enjoyed it... We should make of this an annual event.'

Thirty five and twelve people from St. Clare's and St. Kevin's respectively participated in these days.

These days do not just happen. Much preparation goes into them but this is worth while. The above feedback gives us a good insight into what these days hold for a service community. It brings you together and refreshes you. All find Esker to be an ideal venue for this type of event and never fail to comment on the warmth and welcome of the place.

Parents' days of renewal

These days of renewal for parents who have sons and daughters in the Bruach Na Mara and John Paul Centre community have been offered as 'time out', opportunities to reflect on your journey. The days were tailored to the specific needs of the groups. The focus for the Bruach Na Mara group was on issues related to, *'What will happen my son or daughter when I am gone*?' It was a very pleasant day despite the difficulty of the topic. All enjoyed being together in the lovely setting of Park Lodge, Connemara where a nice meal was served and the Eucharist was celebrated at the end of the day. The service-users of Bruach Na Mara treated their parents to that day out.

We have had similar days for the John Paul Centre parents. These days emanated from a meeting I had with the parent support group where I had been invited to give a presentation on Pastoral Care. Many of the parents present took that opportunity to voice how hurt they had been by the church. They wished for a day of renewal that would allow them to recharge the batteries. So far, two of these days, 'Time out Just for Me' have been offered with a clear focus on themselves rather than their children. They included time to explore their own journey as parent and carers through times of sharing, guided imagery, and liturgy.

Time out with Zacheus

These two days of fun and exploration around the story of Zacheus, included a very moving reconciliation service. The input given by Michael Morris and the type of music and chanting he shared with us and got us to practise, was seen by some as far-fetched, but by others as a very new and challenging experience. A colleague speech therapist described his method and teaching of chanting of sounds rather than words, as *'most appropriate, affirming, comforting and uplifting for people with a learning disability who would find it difficult to remember and sing the words of a song or hymn.'* Perhaps service-users, more than staff, welcomed this new experience with much openness. They commented on how they liked the sounds and the movements that accompanied them.

"Ar Scáth A Chéile" weekend retreats

Ar Scáth A Chéile retreats are an important development for the pastoral programme. They provide a unique experience for people with an intellectual disability and their friends. The focus is aptly captured in the name which was given to the project by the first retreat team: *Ar Scáth A Chéile* weekend. The inspiration, an old Irish saying '*Ar scáth a chéile a mhaireann na daoine*' ('People have to depend on each other to survive') evokes very well this weekend journey undertaken in pairs – a person with a learning disability and a friend. The experience and sharing is rich, nobody is lost in the group and all can count on the gentle and discreet support of a caring and dynamic facilitating team.

These weekends are built around a theme which we explore in pairs and in groups as we engage in discussion groups, drama, art, and outside activities, and take part in liturgies. The Saturday night party which lasts late into the night, is a great time for letting our hair down, enjoying a drink, doing a party piece, and just relaxing in good company.

As '*Ar Scáth A Chéile*' becomes more established we are hopeful that our bank of friends will increase and that the contacts made on the occasion of these weekends will develop and that friendship will grow among the participants. Already some people have made special efforts to keep in contact with those they have accompanied. The get-together/fund raisers which all help in support of *Ar Scáth A Chéile,* provide opportunities for participants to meet again. In fact I have just learned that a young man, who accompanied a service-user from the After-care programme and who has no family support, had invited him to spend Christmas with him and his family.

Fund-raising/reunion events are an important dimension of *Ar Scáth A Chéile*; they serve to build a community awareness and provide a pleasant social evenings. The profits allow us to offer support to those whose only obstacle to coming is financial pressure (This can be the case for both people with a disability and the companions) and cover many other additional costs. The support received from Fr. Johnny Dogherty of Esker Retreat house is very much appreciated as we are aware that much effort goes into providing *Ar Scáth A Chéile* with a great welcome and service at a very reasonable price.

Some comments from the participants:

I liked the way the whole programme was organised; nothing was rushed. I had plenty of time with my companion, with the group, and still I had time on my own.'

'...The journey was well worthwhile.'

'A most enlightening weekend.'

'It was a great weekend for me.'

'The party was beautifully prepared.'

'...to sum up, it was brilliant.'

Sunset retreats

These days of renewal are organised especially for people of retiring age. As with all our other events these are tailored to the needs of the participants. Here the pace is much slower and the day shorter to ensure that nobody gets too tired or overwhelmed by too active a programme. The style of the day is more traditional in content to respect the expression of faith that is familiar to this age group. It is hoped that in the future we will see many more of them as there is now in our services, a greater awareness and respect for the specific needs of people who have entered into this retiring phase of their lives.

Jean Vanier's visit to Galway

Jean Vanier, the founder of the L'Arche communities and Faith and Light was the guest of our Services from the 18th to the 21st of March, 1996.

These four days of festival which brought together service users, members of staff, families, and friends, and many others from the general public proved to be a wonderful time of renewal for all. Three hundred and fifty people gathered for a one-day conference at the John Paul Centre, and two hundred and fifty participants attended the three-day retreat '*Our sacred Journey*' held at Kilcornan, Clarinbridge.

Jean inspired, challenged and affirmed us in our efforts to build a community where through the relationships we share, crossing the disability divides, we can genuinely nourish each other's lives and celebrate each other's gifts. What was lived during these days witnessed to this in many moving ways.

Jean's talks and presence were of course central to these events, but everybody's contribution, people with an intellectual disability, members of staff, friends of the services, and all those who came with an open heart and entered into the mood of the event, helped to make it a celebratory as well as a reflective experience.

Pilgrimages

Going on a pilgrimage is a style of devotion which is still very much alive in Ireland, and one that many service users and members of staff enjoy making on a seasonal basis. Many of our Community Programmes include going to Knock in their yearly calendar and, 'make a great day out of it.' A few years ago the services used to gather there in large numbers. At present the pastoral programme facilitates a different style of pilgrimage; having abandoned these huge gatherings for more intimate ones where only a certain number of participants representing a centre attend the day if the event has a regional dimension.

Much care is put into hosting the day and preparing the liturgy to make sure that it will be an uplifting one for the participants and something to remember for a long time.

So in groups of various sizes, people have gone on pilgrimage to places like Ballintubber, Croagh Patrick, Mac Dara Island and the Burren. These are deeply anchored in the Irish tradition and like all pilgrimages hold a high sensorial dimension.

Mac Dara Island pilgrimage

Going to Mac Dara Island was a unique experience for the six people who made the pilgrimage, the language, the sea, the boat, the oratory, the picnic on the Island, and so on. If our presence touched as many people as we were told, the non-patronising help we got for getting in and out of the boats was for us too a very affirming experience.

Ballintubber pilgrimage

Ballintubber (site of an ancient abbey) which offers a wonderful welcome from the local community, has much to be seen in and around the abbey. The last pilgrimage our services held there was a real festival of faith with much "*craic agus ceol agus ethos*" (good fun, music, and ethos) for the 170 people who were there. Many were very moved by the liturgy which celebrated the gifts that we share in our communities. During the liturgy, when the juggler juggled in from off the altar, we all offered in prayer all that we were best at and on that day this certainly included our joy of being together – 'Tears came to my eyes when I saw this; I was very moved.'

Croagh Patrick Pilgrimage

The Croagh Patrick (a mountain which is the focus of a yearly national pilgrimage) two-day pilgrimage was on a much smaller scale. It gathered sixteen climbers from Clarenmore who excelled themselves in their attempt to make the top of the mountain on a beautiful day. Some had brought us sticks from Kerry for the climb a couple of months before the actual date. This is an indication of how excited people were about this trip.

> '*I cannot believe that my son did it, when I think that he always complains about going for a stroll*' (A mother).

St. Clare's and St. Kevin's Pastoral sessions

I have been meeting with these two groups on a weekly basis for two years. The aim of these sessions is to provide a space away from the busy life of the day centres, where the groups share an experience of faith and receive nourishment by what is lived. The groups have barely changed since the beginning. It was felt that continuity would yield much fruit, and would allow the participants to get to know each other better in this catechetical context, and grow together in their understanding of the space that we create together.

Meeting once a week with these groups has been a huge commitment for me. But how rewarding for all of us. The 'outside facilitation' allows the members of staff who are present there in a supportive role to still enter personally in this faith journey. I see my commitment to these groups as a statement and as a sign – that none of us, regardless of disabilities, should be excluded from the possibilities of growing in our faith and the love of God, and that it is possible to find the means of support for this journey.

> 'There is no doubt that this is a valuable and developing opportunity that has not been presented in this way before and they are keen to see it develop further' (Team Leader).

Liturgical year and Seasonal Celebrations

A wide range of activities, liturgies and celebrations punctuate our seasonal and liturgical calendar. They include Reconciliation service, Advent and Christmas celebrations, Lenten and Easter liturgies, Inter-centre Passover meals, and Lunch time reflections. Some of these happen during working hours while the others take place at evening time. The first one gathered a larger number of people mainly in centres, while the second tends to create more intimate spaces where the atmosphere is more conducive for sharing and relaxation.

Several evenings of reflection and get together have been organised for different groups in both Fáilte House (Galway) and The Elms (Castlerea). The aim of the evening is to provide a time of prayer and fellowship in a warm and welcoming atmosphere.

In Castlerea, service-users have formed a small pastoral committee I meet with for the preparation of these events which might coincide, although not automatically, with a liturgical time, a birthday, or an anniversary. So together we try to articulate the why of our get together. Then we prepare the music, a text to reflect on, a ritual to perform to help us anchor what we are saying and celebrating. And finally, we plan the party and decide on who is going to be invited to come along for the night.

These nights are an ideal time for people to get together. There is usually no hurry and it breaks the routine of residential life. Evenings have focused on: Lent and Easter, Advent and Christmas, story telling, art, pottery and prayer, creation, relationship, and grief.

"Memories of You"

November and the start of the Christmas season often remind us of loved ones who have passed away. It can be a very difficult time for some people who experience loneliness or have not been given the chance to express their grief. 'Memories of You' is a time set aside to safely share memories of those loved ones and find a listening among others who might share the same journey. The approach is symbolic, and working hard from evocations, one comes in touch with the deep feelings which are there and want to be expressed. It is a sound, a smell, a texture, a colour which suddenly opens for you the memory chest... 'You're crying George!', 'I remember the smell of my mother's cooking... Now I have no one left.'

Nobody said 'don't cry'; all those present had cried before. Nobody ventured a vain word of comfort; the presence and the silence of friends who understood, was everything. We all broke a dried piece of stick; It cracks... It's what we felt in our broken hearts!

A time comes during the evening when we learn to close the memory box, find peace and offer peace. It is the time of Faith when the tradition carries you beyond the grave, beyond the cries. We light a candle. Holding it in our hands we walk on the autumn leaves with sticks cracking under our footstep and leave it there on the ground, close to the icon. A warm flame, hands holding tight and a prayer. We go on living. It is time for a cup of tea.

Before John's mother joined us for that cup of tea, Peter brought her to the chapel where we had the ritual. She was moved by what was there and watched where she put her feet. '*You can walk on it, Mother, it cracks like in our hearts. That's the candle for Dad.*'

Harvest Festivals

Many people have, at this stage, participated in Harvest Festivals which have taken place in various venues in our services for several years now. These are great times of celebration, days when we stop for a while and just enjoy ourselves and be thankful to God and each other for what we live throughout the year. We honour each other when we take this time to say who we are and what we do, and find ways of sharing all of this with others. All centres do not produce goods, but this does not prevent the hosting communities in any case from being thankful for something important they may have lived during the year. For example Kilcornan Services produced a very moving mime with the young people from the parish of Ballybane, whom they had got to know during their summer project. The Bruach Na Mara celebration which focused on the sea had a very different tone, but was equally very enjoyable and inspiring. Orchard Centre brought us to Coole Park for thanksgiving around the theme of 'Creation'.

Faith and Light

The Faith and Light movement, a sister movement of L'Arche, provides a powerful model of how community can be built around people with an intellectual disability. These communities gather parents, their sons/daughters with an intellectual disability, and friends. They provide peer support on the one hand, but are also space where support can grow from the larger community. This movement has grown in Ireland over the last few years with 25 communities scattered around the country. Several people from our Services are members of the Galway Faith and Light community.

PASTORAL AWARENESS WORKSHOPS

The following workshops were designed to promote awareness and understanding of Pastoral care.

A common thread to those, the 'come and see' experiential model which has already been articulated above, bore much fruit and allowed the participants to have a rich experience and articulate for themselves the nature of a pastoral dimension.

The evaluation forms which have been returned, confirmed us in our choice for more 'experiential' rather than 'academic' styles of workshops, and showed people's enthusiasm for renewing such experiences and making it available to others.

Pastoral Care in context

This workshop was offered to all centres and areas of Galway and Roscommon as an opportunity of gaining a better understanding of what a pastoral dimension could be about in the context of our services. Many of those attending had already been involved in the organisation of retreats and liturgies, and had therefore much experience to share in the discussion.

These two days were a time of reflection on the Brothers of Charity ethos, the 'journey that we share', the need to 'take care' of oneself and each other, and finally, celebration. Thirty eight people, member of staff and service users, attended the two days

A follow-up day, after three months, gave the participants an opportunity to evaluate what they had lived a few months earlier, address the important issues that had arisen from the feedback, look at the richness and difficulties they had encountered in organising such an event since the previous workshop, and to share in future planning.

'Esker Fest'

Forty-five people from the Brothers of Charity Community Programmes for Adults came to Esker for three days of togetherness, friendship, fun and celebration as the only agenda. The days were action-packed with a great choice of activities: T-shirt making, pottery, badge making, drama, and dough modelling. With some events that gathered the whole group such as: the guided nature walk and slide show with Gordon D'Arcy, the sports afternoon, the party, and the times of prayer and reflection, and tapestry making. The reflections of participants included the following,

> 'I felt good and Happy in Esker after my illness.'
>
> 'It was a great idea to be there for two nights as there was no rushing, everybody felt relaxed.'
>
> 'Made new friends...'
>
> I found being in the little church very moving.'
>
> 'This should become an annual event in the pastoral calendar.'

Inverin weekend *(for members of staff and families)*

This was a loosely structured weekend away just to be together and get to know each other better. Art sessions and games were organised with the children, sharing and a time of prayer happened spontaneously around the fire in the evening.

Weekend breaks *(for service-users)*

Within the context of the *CÁIRDE* pilot project, the pastoral programme was able to offer service-users of Clarenmore a series of 'weekends with a difference.'

These weekends with a difference included time for reflection and discussion, prayer, touring, and a celebratory meal in which all had input from the planning of the menu to the cooking and preparation of a beautiful dinner table.

These weekends were rated very highly when it came to the evaluation. For daily attenders to Clarenmore they offered something they had never before experienced.

All weekends away were followed by a 'Photo evening', an opportunity to talk about our favourite moments and create mementos and a way of sharing memories for people with impaired verbal skills. From the large number of photos that was made available all participants could express their own story of the weekend as they filled in an album they brought home to share with others.

A Parent wrote,

> '*My son really enjoyed the Inverin weekend with the trip to Aran... He enjoyed being away from home and away from family life for a change*'
> (More weekend opportunities were asked for).

There are so many other projects which belong to this section but they cannot all be described here. They include many outings in small groups or on a one-to-one basis, thanks to volunteers, evening socials and dances, and trips to shows.

The Arts on the pastoral programme

The arts have made a significant contribution in the development of the pastoral programme. Music, drama, art and crafts always find their place at one time or another on the occasion of retreats, workshops, ongoing catechetical programmes, and celebrations. They act as a wonderful leveller of relationships when both service-users and members of staff engage together in a project, such as making a banner, a collage, a piece of weaving, or drama, pottery, singing, or drumming. The arts, it is well known, hold great potential in the area of personal development. They bring you beyond words, to the heart of human experience and ultimately to the symbolic.

Art Sessions at Fáilte House

The pastoral care programme has occasionally organised for formal art sessions to be facilitated at Fáilte House. These have been primarily offered to service-users who were interested in these, and had no such options in their centre. The original vision had been to organise these events at the

Galway Arts Centre or another studio. Unfortunately, our financial resources made us settle for Fáilte House which was not the ideal option. Nevertheless, this venue provided us with a space where the atmosphere differed sufficiently from that of the centre and allowed people to relax and open up to the session process. To the joy of all parties these warm painting hours refused to become art therapy sessions.

Drama

We can look with much pleasure at the impact that drama has had over the past two years on the lives of some twenty five people, who Monday after Monday, get together for a couple of hours of fun, relaxation and exploration of who we are as individuals and members of various communities.

This ongoing programme has opened many doors for people – the doors of their workshops, the doors of their creative energies and imagination, the doors of the Druid Theatre, and the doors of their heart and of their emotions. Through these workshops, many in the group have acquired a more positive self image and a greater self confidence. Some people have even pushed hard and used their self advocacy skills to secure their drama sessions!

The Drummer Boy

The Drummer Boy was a unique drama experience involving twenty five people, service-users and members of staff from four adult centres, who met over a period of 12 weeks before Christmas to create the story and characters of a very human journey from the mundane to the wonderful, from poor self image to trust in one's gift.

After many rehearsals, the cast finally presented a humorous and moving production of *The Drummer Boy* (two performances which were sold out on both nights) at the Druid Theatre in Galway. There were many wonderful moments of audience and cast interaction and a sense of real community integration for the cast, their families and friends.

This thought-provoking production 'made' Christmas for many of those who participated in the production, but also for those who had the privilege of witnessing this new departure.

Music

Exploring the healing power of sound and music led us to a workshop for which no musical or singing ability were really required from the participants. The richness of the day was in the gathering of both staff and service-users on the same footing and everybody's openness to a very new experience. Chanting! Singing the scales! Drumming! Dancing from Sufi, Native American, and Irish traditions, discovery of new sounds and rhythms were on the programme. Once again this workshop which was facilitated by Michael Morris, and attended by twenty eight participants revealed the power of sound and music and its potential for personal development.

Deirdre Stephens, Music Therapist, has also facilitated sessions on the occasion of workshops or summer projects. An **African Day** was the occasion of discovering new rhythms, dances and stories for service users, staff and youth from the Ballybane area on a Saturday, an old Romanesque church in Kilcornan, St. Cornan's, has also been a wonderful venue for hosting small musical events, carols, sing-along with Debbie Moore and Friends, and '**Celtic spirituals**' with Carmel Boyle.

COMMUNITY AWARENESS

This is a very exciting area to which this programme has also made some contribution, the main ones being as follows.

Three holiday projects in conjunction with Kilcornan and Ballybane youth group.

This project, run for three years in a row, was a great success from both the residents' and staff of Kilcornan at the Maples, and the Ballybane Youth point of view. It was run in conjunction with Debbie Moore, former pastoral worker of Ballybane parish.

This disability awareness and personal development programme for youth, turned out to be a wonderful summer project for everyone involved. The youth and a very creative action-packed programme brought great life to Kilcornan and gave the residents involved in the week many new experiences. All engaged in drama, music, arts and craft, pottery, sports, mixed group swimming gala, day trips to Clare including picnics, and meals out. Following this programme, two young people came back to Kilcornan on a weekly basis for the rest of the summer. Both residents and youth expressed the wish of meeting each other again. This was facilitated on the occasion of a Harvest Festival and three Saturday events.

There is much support in Kilcornan for such a project to be run on an ongoing basis, but unfortunately at the present time, the absence of a contact person in Ballybane parish and limited resources, both human and financial, force us to leave this summer project on one side for the moment.

School based disability awareness

Services like ours have a responsibility to support religious education teachers in their endeavours to develop disability awareness programmes and a more caring attitudes towards those whom society tends to marginalise.

I met with the teachers of two transition classes a number of times, presented the programme 'Breakthrough' and facilitated the first session. This creative and flexible programme designed by St. Michael's House in Dublin is excellent for schools which do not have the opportunity of visiting a centre on a regular basis. In this case both groups visited our services at some stage and organised a return visit.

This is an area which deserves more attention than it is given, although I am aware that many centres welcome students for varying lengths of time and that occasional speakers have addressed classrooms when the occasion arose. Religion and transition classes seem to welcome us particularly, as do youth groups in parish communities.

Future Developments and Challenges

Paradoxically, this Pastoral Programme which has developed from the margin of the organisation, has found its home at the very heart of the services, its vision and its people.

If, on the one hand, this chapter attests to the vitality of the programme and its potential, on the other hand, it also points towards areas which need attention, and which if addressed, will allow the programme to develop further.

Challenges and Recommendations

There is an urgent need for this programme to be formally integrated into the Services and to be given the recognition it needs which will enable it to develop further. This includes,

1. the appointment of a pastoral co-ordinator to the Galway Services (now implemented,
2. the preparation of a pastoral policy document to be endorsed by the Directorate,
3. the development of an organisational structure which will facilitate the implementation of the pastoral care policy,
4. the formation of regional and local pastoral teams,
5. the securing of formal support from programme teams for pastoral team members,
6. the development of a greater awareness of what the pastoral programme can offer,
7. the research into, and design of liturgical and catechetical material,
8. the organising of staff training for facilitation of pastoral sessions,
9. the encouraging of better interaction between administrative services and service-users,
10. the developing of a volunteer programme,
11. the looking at the possibility of renewing and developing the *CÁIRDE* project and the appointment of a Volunteer Co-ordinator,

12. the fostering of staff renewal in a more systematic way in an effort to address burn-out,
13. the making of training provisions which reflect the needs and wishes of service users in the area of personal development,
14. the initiating of parish-based disability awareness programmes which could lead to developing better community integration and the implementation of a community based volunteering programme or the setting up of new Faith and Light communities, and
15. the hosting in Galway of a conference which would offer a vision and a forum for service-users, organisations and communities which seek to include the needs and wishes of people with a learning disability in their pastoral programmes.

All these recommendations are worth serious consideration. The first ones if taken on board will secure the development of this programme and will re-energise all those in the services who wish to lend this programme their goodwill and commitment so that, with the service-users, all that has been initiated may be further developed to everybody's benefit.

CONCLUSION

The chapter has its limits, words, black ink on a white page, no colours, no smells, no candles and above all no faces... I have written about celebrating, about making sense of our experiences, about our vision, our needs to be nourished and to be inspired again. I hope the future will give us the opportunity to present it again in an inclusive, creative and festive way to truly celebrate what we set out to do, to re-kindle the pastoral dimension in our services.
Today the words and comments I often hear or read on evaluation sheets contrast greatly with those I heard in the early days of my appointment. They speak of,

'feeling renewed',
'getting to know each other better',
'having a sense of belonging',
'reconnecting with people I hadn't seen in a long time',

'the togetherness at mass and at the party', and
'enjoying accompanying and being a friend to John.'

REFERENCE

Pottebaum, G.A. (1992). *The Rites of People: Exploring the Ritual Character of Human Experience*. Washington DC: PastoralPress.

Biographical Note

Claude Madec was born in Brittany, France in 1958 and came to Galway in 1980. From the very beginning of his time in Ireland, he has been associated with people with an intellectual disability their families and Services.
In 1993 he was appointed to the Brothers of Charity Services in Ireland to co-ordinate the rekindling and development of a pastoral dimension. His involvement with the Faith and Light movement both nationally and internationally is an important influence in his work. He has facilitated many workshops in Ireland and abroad. This article gives an insight into his approach to pastoral care in the special needs community.

Claude holds a BA from NUI Galway and an MA in Pastoral Studies from La Salle University, Pennsylvania USA. He is married with two children.

9   CIRCLES OF SUPPORT

Mandy Neville and Barry McIver

Introduction

> *I have lived in the flats (a tower block) for six years, go to church each week, go to the day centre Monday to Friday, but I'm lonely, so very, very lonely...*

These were the words of a middle aged woman with learning difficulties, uttered between sobs as she began to tell her story. Such feelings are echoed over and over again in the many stories we have shared with people who experience enduring feelings of exclusion.

Isolation and loneliness can provide the most significant disability for people and yet there have been few attempts and little provision of funding to invest in ensuring that disabled people, and people with learning difficulties, have the opportunities and support to make fulfilling and sustainable natural friendships. Circles Network, now the leading UK organisation providing assistance for people to be included through circles of support in ordinary community life, set out from its inception in 1993 to concentrate effort on the complex subject of friendship and love.

This chapter will focus on a social organisation known as a circle of support, which undermines isolation and loneliness. It will describe the historical context of the development of circles and draw a wider picture for the reader of the ways that exclusion might be challenged. In the process, it will encourage practitioners to examine the prejudice, isolation and indifference experienced by people with disabilities. Throughout, there will be illustrations of real examples of how lives can change in circles of support, not only for those for whom the circle is a focus, but also for those who are participants. The chapter will conclude with a description of Circles Network, a company of people who work to link together and co-ordinate hundreds of circles in the United Kingdom, and beyond.

The context and history

The notion of a circle of support is essentially simple, to help someone who is, or is at risk of being, marginalised establish a personal social network. In practice however, when people have experienced broken relationships and systems, which congregate, segregate and disempower, creating such a network requires deliberate action to make opportunities for natural relationships to develop.

One of the earliest leaders in this work, Judith Snow, suggests that *'A circle is a vehicle which is joyous and fun'* a description bound to entice the reader on to further exploration. Judith created her own circle of support, which is the first documented experience of this kind, at the age of 31, when in her job as Director of the centre for students with disabilities at York University, Toronto, Canada, she found herself to be extremely isolated and struggling with ill health. Required to live in a nursing home through the nature of her severe physical impairments and the lack of appropriate resources, she found it impossible to hold down a tough job whilst enduring an institutional regime of care. Her colleague, Marsha Forest, grew concerned and encouraged Judith to call together a group of the people she knew who cared for her. That first circle where Judith shared her feelings of despair was known as the Joshua Committee because it broke down the barriers to community and began to let her in. The story is told in greater detail in Pearpoint (1992) and further in Snow (1994).

Marsha Forest, Jack Pearpoint and Judith Snow went on to develop the notion of circles of support (or circles of friends) and to expand on their learning about the inclusion of all people, however different, in ordinary community life. From Canada, the learning spread southwards to Connecticut where an organisation called *Communitas* (Latin for community) formed in 1987 to work initially with five disabled people and their families. These five circles of support were so successful that they began to change the wider social structure in the neighbourhoods where they formed. Each circle had its own impact, changing church communities, housing initiatives, care arrangements and school and transport systems. This work is recorded in the book: *What are we learning about circles of support?* (Beeman, Ducharme and Mount, 1988).

Communitas is now an international networking organisation which links together people who are committed to enriching communities, neighbourhoods, associations, schools and workplaces through the full inclusion and participation of disabled people. It was through their help and guidance that the first circle of support began here in Britain in 1989.

The experience of Judith Snow and *Communitas* began to make and impact on people in the United Kingdom who realised that their own work could be enhanced by circles of support. New opportunities for friendship and action had significant implications for both practitioners and disabled people and their families, and in 1989 an initial circle in Bristol was started.

Susie's circle is documented in the book entitled, *Circles of Support, Building Inclusive Communities* (Wetheimer, 1995). The powerful experience she shared with her circle members who were ordinary people she had met through her closest friend, Many Neville, allowed her to take control and make huge changes in her life. This in turn led to a strong commitment by some of her circle to open up similar opportunities for others. In the space of a few years, she had moved out of a 24-place hostel into a house which she was involved in choosing. She re-connected with a man she had shared a forbidden relationship with (forbidden by the staff of the hostel) and eventually married him. She gained access to further education in a mainstream college having previously only experienced a hospital special school. She left the large day centre which she had always disliked and took on part-time employment in three different settings. Her social life blossomed and she developed strong enduring friendships. Although her physical and sensory impairments and her learning difficulties were still a constant feature of hr life, her self-confidence and personal sense of fulfilment took a dramatic climb. Eventually, her reconnection with her family who, on professional advice, had given her up to care in a hospital when she was a young child, resulted in the ultimate inclusion for her. It provided the warmth, the care and the life, which cannot possibly be duplicated in any institutional setting.

Other circles of support very quickly sprang up, fuelled with great enthusiasm and life. It was apparent that the learning resulting from these early circles of support in Bristol and for the growing number of participants, required articulation and verification if the notion of circles was to develop further in the United Kingdom. It was agreed, after some debate as to whether the American experience would 'travel' (Cox and Neville, 1995), to hold a national conference in Bristol in March 1992 focused on circles of support to which *Communitas* was invited to play a leading role. A result of this conference was a determination to create an organisation, which would work to identify, promote and develop a national focus for circles of support. Circles Network emerged as a direct result of this and is described below.

By 1995, *Communitas* went on to move from their office base to take over a busy main street Post Office in Manchester, Connecticut. They wanted to reach out beyond communities of disabled people and workers in human service systems, and felt that by investing locally in their own community they would explore what it would actually take to develop inclusive communities where everyone is valued simply for their worth as human beings. The Post Office offers a central point in a neighbourhood, and the intention is to inform and influence customers' thinking on an everyday basis. The Post Office is staffed by disabled and non-disabled workers, it has a shop which sell literature, cards, candles and gifts and through various activities organised for this base, people are invited to celebrate difference through experiencing opportunities to meet people from all social backgrounds. The *Communitas* team continue to write and share their learning at conferences and workshops both in the United States of America and abroad.

From exclusion to inclusion

The basis of circles is essentially simple; to provide a catalyst and a conduit for people who are isolated by difference to find a place in the community at large. Most people have felt the pain of exclusion at some time in their lives and can relate to the feelings experienced through marginalisation. For people who have profound and long term experiences of exclusion the circle of support can provide a safe place to address the hurt and begin to change the patterns.

McKnight and Kretzman (1993) have argued that post war society has asset-stripped communities by isolating disabled people. This, they maintain, creates the stereotype belief that disabled people have nothing to offer. Institutional incarceration feeds the myth that disabled people are to be feared, which in turn, often leads to loathing. The resulting dependency culture has limited the ability of communities to solve their own difficulties, preferring instead the specialist services of the care and social work industry. This has suppressed any natural desire for self-help to flourish, particularly in the deprived inner city areas. Bringing people back into communities, as determined by the Community Care Act (1989) is not an end in itself. It is not possible for people to shake off their misconceptions without the opportunity to repair the cultural divides that have inevitably occurred. Until people have the opportunity for proximity and reciprocity in their relationships, true and meaningful inclusion will remain an ideological dream. The major key to bridging the gulf of discrimination is to invest in the belief that everyone, regardless of background, has gifts to share. This can be explored in great detail if each circle of support is considered to be a microcosm of community.

It may not always be easy to find the gifts in people who have learned to communicate through aggressive, difficult or compulsive behaviours. It will take a great deal of empathy and tolerance to look beneath the layers to discover the person within. In many people it is easy to celebrate the gifts which they share. It may be an engaging smile, a passion for life or any of a range of talents.

When asked why she had stopped going to the day centre, Doris Clark said that it was too big and that she didn't feel like a person there. Several years of the same time wasting activities, in a bleak and miserable environment, had certainly taken its toll on her self-confidence. With the help of her circle she began to devote her time to undertake some voluntary work. She worked at first for two different organisations and has progressed in just two short years to the position of Chair of the Management Board of one, where she speaks at meetings, organises events, supervises paid workers and signs the cheques. In the second, she now holds a part time paid position as Development Officer, dealing with enquiries, co-leading courses and training events, and dealing with a range of administrative tasks. At the day centre she was a passive recipient and hardly even cared whether she washed before going in. She still talks with tears in her eyes about how insignificant and lonely she felt in those days. Even though she liked some of the staff, she felt that they held all the power; they were the important people at the centre. Now she takes pride in the way she looks, she has meaningful purpose every morning when she awakes and loves to talk with her friends about the work she so enjoys.

The whole concept of inclusion is based on a paradigm shift, a cultural change, which is underpinned by the belief that all people, however labelled, have the right to participate and belong in communities. We propose that people should be surrounded by friends and family, and involved in a whole range of relationships; and that they should take appropriate control in the service from which they require assistance. Inclusion means the direct opposite of the exclusion and oppression prevalent in societies for centuries on which our human services are largely based. This concept is aligned with the social model of disability, which projects the theory that it is society which disables rather than any condition or impairment, which the person may experience (Oliver, 1980). This model urges society to change in attitudes and in systems, structures and environments which prevent people with impairments participating through political, legislative and economic influences. In contrast, the medical model of disability focuses on what is perceived to be wrong with the person. The medical model of disability has led to a wide range of practices which have sanctioned the use of medical and surgical intervention, aversive treatments and a trend in looking for a cure or a method of fixing and changing the person. Guided by the social model and inclusion paradigm, people are challenged to accept and celebrate difference and to radically change practices which disempower and marginalise individuals, and focus instead on ensuring the achievement of dignity and respect for all people in a culture based on human civil rights.

Snapshots of circles in progress

A circle of support enhances rather than replaces the need for high quality human services. In many situations, the person and his or her circle, persuades the service provider to be more effective and more flexible in their response to the needs of support identified. A case manager who is prepared to listen to the views of circle members will find that much of the planning and strategic thinking has been conducted in natural environments with a distinct lack of bureaucracy.

When Arran's Mother was considering with professionals what may happen to her son when at nineteen he was due to leave the special school he had attended, his prospects looked pretty bleak. A placement in the special needs unit of the nearest day centre, occasional weeks of respite care in the challenging behaviour unit fifteen miles away, and a place at the local Gateway club one evening a week were the key ingredients to his future plan. When Arran and his Mother talked with his circle about what he may do, the list was much greater.

Sunday mornings tinkering with cars at the garage where his uncle works could provide opportunities to further his interest in mechanics and driving. His fascination with fast cars and motorbikes may be a link to future employment and leisure pursuits. Monthly weekend stays with friends Bill and Jo, and with cousins Kirsty and Jim, would give mother and son the breaks they needed on a regular basis, which would make a real difference to easing tensions without painful, unhappy separations. A place at the local community college with one-to-one support would give him the chance to study for some basic qualifications. It would also create opportunities to spend time with other young people from his neighbourhood. He decided he would like to go bowling regularly with his friend Chris. Nasseem, one of his neighbours suggested Arran might like to try go-karting with him at a Saturday morning class.

Funding which has been allocated to provide the day centre placement would, if re-directed, buy him the services of two part-time personal assistants who could work with Arran from home assisting him to get out and about locally and to try out a range of jobs and activities.

When Andrew Williams's circle began, he was living in Wales with his mother and father. He had always been happy with his life, but then, as his brother noted, no-one had ever previously had high aspirations for his future. What people discovered was that Andrew had probably always had leadership skills – he had simply never been in a position to use them. Recently he decided to walk in the Himalayas, and with the circle, planned what proved to be a hugely successful trip. At regular circle meetings he is able to plan for his future, helping his family come to terms with thinking about what may happen if he decides to leave home. Together they can build safeguards which enable him to take risks and continue to explore the adventurous characteristics which are clearly significant. He has become much more assertive and is intentionally building a lifestyle similar to that of other single men in their late twenties.

Control in the circle must always remain with the focus person, and he or she will determine the pace of the initial start up and all ongoing progress. One family took three years to actually begin their circle. There were so many issues to consider, so many other people to think of. At first, they found it difficult to admit that they needed additional help to change their daily patterns of life, and then there were times they feared the changes which would inevitably occur. People worried, inevitably, schooled as we all are in systems which categorise and label people into groups, that the circle approach would not fit their individual and particular needs.

One of the nightmares expressed by parents of children and young people with learning difficulties, is that they will grow up without any real friendships. Most of us take for granted that the children we care about get invited to parties, to sleep over at a friend's house, to receive birthday greetings and invitations to 'hang out' with youngsters of a similar age. When Becky became fourteen, that picture became a reality too. Her parents had not realised quite how much they had been grieving for those simple acts of acceptance and warmth, which had not been a feature of their eldest daughter's life. Her circle of support began when she was twelve but it did take a further two years before she had a solid group of teenagers belonging in a full capacity.

The circle, which was originally set up for her, developed to surround the whole family eventually. The teenagers met with the rest of the group, and in addition, set up a sub-circle because they wanted to meet much more frequently as they had a lot of fun things to explore.

When Becky learned to use Facilitated Communication, it was discovered that she could read and was more intelligent than had previously been recognised. Her growing ability to communicate and her opportunities to have people with whom to express herself, coupled with some new understanding about how movement difficulties affected her, led to a massive reduction in the challenges she posed. For her family, what transpired was a new rhythm, a different way of including Becky which met everyone's needs more effectively. The circle also brought their extended family and whole assortment of friends, much closer to them all.

Issues for circles to consider

It is not possible to describe a definitive list of guidelines for circle building. There is no 'quick fix'. The unique relationships within each individual circle are the reason why no template could be crafted. As the focus person begins to find their own power, supported in friendship by the people they have asked to be with them through this journey of inclusion, so they direct the group's efforts in their own particular style.

The major difference most circle members remark on, is the way the focus person develops a range of relationships, which vary in depth. This includes the kinship and anchorage of friends and family, the intimacy of significant bonds, fellow participants, colleagues, acquaintances, peers and care givers. People aim to change often long standing patterns, where the only people in a person's life are those who are paid to be there. For anyone who has lost sight of ties and connections at a particular point of trauma, it is crucial to rebuild or create a new beginning for strong and desirable friendships. It is sometimes necessary to begin this process before a circle can be formed. Paid staff or professional care-givers can provide a 'bridge' into community using their own personal networks and by linking individuals through their gifts and interests to other people who may well begin to form a natural attachment.

It is crucial, if circles are to really make a difference, for this work to remain outside the domain of professional services. It is not ethical for a service provider to create or develop a circle of support for someone in receipt of their professional services. Inevitably the circle would be compromised and unable to advocate freely on behalf of the person. This would create further unnatural relationships, which would simply reinforce the dependency model inherent in many services. There is however a responsibility for human service providers to ensure that people in their care are given access and full assistance to discover for themselves the range of available support to achieve advocacy and empowerment.

It is surprising how many people agree to become involved in a circle of support when they have a clear understanding of the impact it will have ,not only on the life of the person in the position of asking for help, but also on their own lives. Not everyone will be fully committed but when that does happen the circle makes a great leap forward. A circle of support cannot be forced; individuals must make up their own minds about pursuing this style of community building. For some people the exposure of their personal history and concerns is too great a hurdle to overcome.

In all circles of support people are encouraged to dream. This practice leads us beyond the current reality of daily life to create more fulfilling and exciting expectations. It may be hard for people to imagine anything different, let alone dream. Many parents talk about the shattering of their dreams when their son or daughter was first diagnosed and labelled different. When surrounded by difficulties and nightmares, dreams can seem unattainable. Susie's first dreams were not for the re-unification of her family, it took a long time before she could allow herself that degree of vision. Initially, she dreamt of having her own kettle, a statement which evoked some understanding amongst her friends that she desired the resources to offer and reciprocate hospitality.

Throughout the life of a circle, many issues will arise which need to be addressed. As with any organic process, there is often a feeling of chaos which requires attention. Much of the learning disseminated from different circles will help people to develop strategies for overcoming the multitude of problems posed by any set of human relationships.

Challenging assumptions

An interesting feature of circles can be seen in the way that assumptions about how best to support, let us say, people with learning difficulties in wider society are often challenged. Most people are uncomfortable with those who are different. Often this discomfort is rationalised by the assertion that we must protect people with learning difficulties for their own good. What this implies, of course, is isolation - isolation in the name of safety. This assumption leads directly to isolation, either in the sense of institutionalisation or over protection at home. Circles of support create the safety net for risk-taking and each time a new risk is safely negotiated greater encouragement is generated to renew the risk-taking effort. What is actually happening here, is that safety for the focus person is generated through the successful conclusion of an activity regarded perhaps as very risky. Facing our dragons, being conscious of the nightmares which cause great anxiety and fear, is an important feature of a successful circle of support.

No member of a circle, is of course, immune from similar feelings of fear from similar risks. What is apparent however, is how far such fears recede through collective effort and the recognition that the circle as a community provides support and security for all its members. It is this experience that encourages the growth of mutual trust in the circle; that assists members to lose their fears of risk-taking; that points to the false nature of many of the assumptions of people in general.

Circles Network

In the early days of circle development in the United Kingdom, there was a sense of nervousness; a tension about whether of not the idea would translate across the ocean. It was decided to remain very cautious and contain the Network and the information until there was sufficient evidence to believe in.

What transpired, was that change happened so fast, and so powerfully that people could not possibly keep the idea to themselves. Within the first two years, nine circles of support were established and the members of each of those circles wanted to meet each other and to celebrate the new developments beginning to happen.

The first meeting where all of those circles came together was a real celebration of accomplishments. People still had difficulties of course, and there were major goals set in some circles that would take a long time to achieve, but the belief that this way of walking together, of problem solving, of positive, creative thinking was having an impact on everyone's personal esteem. The early group decided to create an organisation, which would put this work on a public platform and make it available for anyone to access.

Circles Network was formed in 1993 with an educational objective to build inclusive communities through the foundation of circles of support. Based in Bristol, Circles Network registered as a national charity and a limited company, and set out to serve anyone who was experiencing exclusion through learning or mental health difficulties, physical or sensory impairments, or enduring ill health.

The organisation was funded from its inception by the Barrow Cadbury Trust, with the Department of Health supporting the work with a core grant and with project grants. Additional funding comes from donations, small grants, commissioned work with individuals, and from training, conference and consultancy work. We are resolute in our efforts to finance the activities we believe in so strongly. Rapid expansion in the early years meant that hundreds of circles were developing, involving thousands of people across all cultures. Circles seemed to work for people of all ages in a whole variety of circumstances. The learning was overwhelming, as was the demand for information and assistance. As the organisation evolved it was felt that in addition to the development, maintenance and networking of circles of support, there were other specific areas of work which needed intense focus.

Currently, the Network has the following broad aims:

- To develop and sustain circles of support.

- To offer consultancy and training for statutory, voluntary and independent sector services on issues related to inclusion and change.

- To provide and organise individualised support for disabled people and people with learning difficulties living in their own homes in community.

- To establish unique support for parents who have learning difficulties and other impairments who require assistance to parent their children at home.

- To co-ordinate a wide ranging programme of courses, conferences, workshops and events, open to anyone, which expand on learning about inclusion.

- To deliver individualised support for people perceived as challenging who want to live in the community, and

- To facilitate *Partners in Policymaking* - A leadership programme designed to achieve policy and systems change involving disabled people and parents of school age disabled children.

All of this work is underpinned by a strong values base of inclusion and disability equality.

Anyone involved in a circle of support can belong to the Network. Regular gatherings and events are held where people come together to share stories and build on ideas and connections. It is clear that people are finding fulfilment and help through circles of support. There is a noticeable shift away from relationships based on the role of helper and helpee as the group develops its thinking and practice towards becoming a more equal community where difference is valued and celebrated. The Network exists to nurture and promote such values. Our dream of the future is summarised brilliantly by Jill Penman and Pippa Murray (1995) when they report:

*We dream for our children and for
your children - for our children's
children. We dream that children
who are labelled, like our children
are today, will one day be included
without the slightest surprise, debate
or controversy.*

REFERENCES

Beeman, P., Ducharme, G., and Mount, B. (1988). *What are we Learning about Circles of Support?* Manchester, CT: Communitas.

Cox L. and Neville M. (1995). Video; *Circles of Support, Building Inclusive Communities.* Bristol: Circles Network.

Department of Health. (1989). *Caring for People: Community Care in the Next Decade and Beyond.* London: HMSO.

Ludlum, C. (1993). *Tending the Candle: A Booklet for Circle Facilitators.* Manchester, CT: Communitas.

McKnight, J.L. and Kretzman, J.P. (1983) *Building Communities from the Inside out: A Path Toward Finding and Mobilizing a Community's Assets.* Illinois: Centre for Urban Affairs of Policy Research.

Murray, P. and Penman J. (1966). *Let our Children be: A Collection Of Stories.* Sheffield: Parents With Attitude.

Oliver, M. (1990). *The Politics of Disablement.* Basingstoke: TheMacmillan Press Ltd.

Pearpoint, J. (1992). *From Behind the Piano.* Toronto, Ont.: Inclusion Press.

Reiser, R. and Mason, M. (1992). *Disability Equality in the Classroom: A Human Rights Issue.* London: London Education Authority.

Snow, J. (1994). *What's Really Worth Doing and how to Do It.* Toronto Ont.: Inclusion Press.

Wetheimer, A. (1995). *Circles of Support, Building Inclusive Communities.* Bristol: Circles Network.

Biographical Notes

Mandy Nevill is a founder member and the Director of Circles Network and was involved in developing the first circle of support in the United Kingdom. She had worked alongside disabled people and people with learning difficulties all of her working life, first in social work and later in special and then further education and has a personal long-standing commitment to working towards building inclusive communities where everyone belongs. More recently she completed a masters degree in management development and social responsibility, and she enjoys the challenge of leadership through love.

Barry McIver has recently taken early retirement form the position of Chief Executive of a large urban community college following a career in industry, community, and further education in various parts of the United Kingdom. He became involved in Circles Network when invited by his late wife Andrea to help create a circle of friends to support her during her illness and the period up to her premature death. Barry became the Chair of the Board of Trustees and helped set up the organisation in 1993. He remains a member of the Board. His interest in community building and inclusive education is long standing.

10 'WE ARE ONE PEOPLE' PASTORAL SUPPORT IN THE DIOCESE OF ARUNDEL AND BRIGHTON

Julia Granger

In the late 1980s a group of people in the Roman Catholic Diocese of Arundel and Brighton met to talk about their hopes and fears. They were parents whose sons and daughters had learning disabilities, along with friends, clergy and professionals. Inspired by this meeting the Diocese published a pastoral handbook, *'We Are One People'* in 1989, as a first step towards offering practical support to parents and to all people with learning disabilities in the Church. A year later, in 1990, in partnership with the Catholic Children's Society, it set up a new pastoral support service, and I was employed as a Development Worker. The new service was a sign that the local church recognised and accepted its responsibility to enable all of its members to be fully incorporated into the life of the church. But what the task of incorporation would involve had to emerge gradually.

In listening to parents, we heard of their deep sense of isolation, and disconnection from the life of the Church community. In some parishes there were local initiatives offering support, but these were not always widely known. Families who attended Mass regularly could still feel isolated by the needs of their child, and constantly anxious lest they created a disturbance for others. With the move from institutional care to care in the community, parishes were being given greater opportunities to welcome and include people with learning disabilities, but uncertainty or embarrassment often held people back. Some adult Catholics, living in residential homes within a parish came to Mass every Sunday and yet experienced few opportunities to get to know other parishioners. Despite the existence of the Bishops' Guidelines on the reception of Holy Communion, written almost ten years earlier, many people, particularly adults in long-term care, had never received the Sacraments of Eucharist and Confirmation. It was still not universally accepted that those with learning disabilities could receive, and should be prepared for these sacraments.

Likewise, many others were seemingly 'invisible', remaining on the margins of church life, unknown to parish or clergy.

But there were also many signs of hope. There was obvious goodwill on the part of many parishioners and innovative examples of catechesis. Several individuals who served at the altar, or sang in the choir and were active members of their parishes, also happened to have learning disabilities. In a few deaneries, groups of families and friends were meeting regularly to celebrate Mass and offer mutual support, and had been doing so for many years.

However, overall it was a patchy picture, with no effective means of spreading good news from one parish to another. Inevitably, the risk was that good practice only came about because of the enthusiasm and commitment of a particular priest or parishioner, and could quickly vanish if this person moved away.

If any long-term change was to be initiated, which would affect the Diocese as a whole, ways would have to be found to extend the understanding of the wider Catholic community. We needed to respect and respond to people's special needs, and at the same time to appreciate their gifts and potential. It was essential that we gave support to families and to individuals, but we also hoped to establish ways of working which moved beyond simple voluntary work. It was not simply a matter of enabling people to be physically present in our parish communities, but of recognising that each person has a valued place and role, and through these, to contribute to, as well as receiving from the Body of Christ. It was important that those with learning disabilities, and their families, were not just present but strongly connected to others in their parishes.

A PARISH NETWORK

One of the ways we chose to pursue this goal was through building up a diocesan network of parish contacts, or representatives. We aimed to find at least one person in each of the 120 parishes of the Diocese who would have a particular concern for those with learning disabilities and their families.

These representatives would be linked to each other on a deanery basis. Individually they would keep direct contact with the diocesan development worker. The choice of the word 'network' was deliberate. We were not setting out to establish a professional support structure, but something more personal and organic, which would grow in response to, and in relationship with, the people in each individual parish. The parish representative was not expected to be an unpaid social worker or nurse, or an 'expert' who could solve all problems. They were not to take responsibility for all the issues in the parish relating to learning disability. Rather, it was hoped they could act as a bridge, knowing how to put people in touch with appropriate help or advice in the diocese or local area.

The role of the parish representative included the following:

> To act as a signpost, whose presence in the parish acted as witness to the concern of the whole church, and to the value of each person with learning disabilities. He or she would need to know and share the values and principles underpinning this work, namely, that the persons with a learning disability and their families were not to be defined simply as people who need help, but rather as individuals with unique value and dignity, fellow Christians with a share in the mission and life of the Church.

> To act as a friend, who would get to know the families with a child or adult with learning disabilities, and those adults living in residential homes locally who were members of the parish.

> To be informed about what we were trying to do in the Diocese and the events and help available.

> To be a link, who tried to make connections between people, and encourage integration and community building.

These were guidelines, not a blueprint for action. The role was as much to do with attitude as with activity, and with example as with organisation.

We were to find that recruitment was not a simple task. Initially all parish priests were invited to nominate a representative, but as few felt able to do so at this early stage, we began to invite parents, professionals and parishioners to nominate and cajole each other to come forward! They bring a wide range of skills, experiences and hopes to their role. Many of the representatives are parents, with personal experience of bringing up a child with a learning disability. Several others are social workers, nurses, teachers or psychologists and so can bring their particular perspective on learning disability to their parish life. Many more are 'ordinary' parishioners, some with little previous knowledge or experience of learning disability but with a willingness to become involved. Recruitment remains a long-term task, which requires central organisation, as individual representatives leave and new people need to be invited to take part.

Initial training sessions are led by the Diocesan worker on a deanery basis. These address issues of community care policies, and current trends regarding learning disability, as well as Christian responses, and questions of language and attitude. Further training continues through newsletters, bulletins, and an annual conference. There are occasional training days on particular topics. Where possible, parish representatives link with others in their deanery and so can contribute to each other's development and offer more immediate local support.

Parish representatives are encouraged to decide on their own priorities in responding to the needs and hopes which arise in their parishes. Advice and help are offered in identifying these. Each parish is unique in its membership and needs, and each representative equally has his or her own skills, weaknesses and time restraints. Their impact on their parish can therefore vary widely. Some feel that they are primarily a witness, or, a '*voice crying in the wilderness*', as they publicise their presence, but receive little apparent response. Others have made strong personal links with individual families and have a high profile in their community.

Successes are many, though they may seem small, or only of significance to the persons concerned. For instance, in one parish a number of adults, living in a large residential home, were prepared for the sacrament of Confirmation.

They have since become visibly involved in all aspects of parish life, both liturgical and social. In another, a man, previously unknown to the parish, has been enabled to regularly attend Mass. A family has been befriended and offered babysitting help. Adults have joined prayer groups, attended retreats, and been offered holidays with other, non-disabled people their own age. Individual parishioners have discovered new friendships and ways of relating with people they previously feared. Some priests have been invited to explore new ways of communicating the mysteries of faith. In some areas, parish representatives have joined together to organise an occasional 'special' liturgical gathering or Mass. Some parents have found here a level of acceptance they had not found in their own parishes. Such groups can be of value in helping individuals re-integrate into their parish, and can provide opportunities for real friendships to be made, which continue beyond the group. They can encourage clergy to consider more accessible liturgies and learn new ways of communication. However, such groups can also have disadvantages if they become the main focus of parish representatives' or the church's attention, creating a separate community within the church. The challenge we face is to offer this level of support and acceptance within every parish community, and at the same time to be prepared, as individual Christians, to learn and change. In this way our church becomes truly accessible and inclusive of all people.

Each success, however small, is never insignificant. Even the smallest of steps takes us all nearer to our destination, and indicates to others the destination we seek. We need to remember that we are creating a network of personal support and individual relationships, not a separate organisation for meeting needs. The latter is the responsibility of the whole parish. Our role is to help and encourage them to carry this out. Such a perspective is essential if we are not to be overwhelmed by the sense of what is still undone. Many parishes are still without a representative, many families continue to feel alienated from the church, and adults can easily be patronised and tolerated, rather than welcomed as fellow parishioners. Yet, as a Diocese, we have a sense of closer involvement, as people with learning disabilities are more visibly present and active at both parish and diocesan level.

DEVELOPMENTS FROM THE PARISH NETWORK

To support and supplement the work of the parish representatives' network, we have offered various Diocesan-wide initiatives, ranging from holidays, training workshops and conferences to catechetical formation and retreats. These have encouraged parishes to develop their thinking in new ways and have introduced many new people to our work. Most of these initiatives originally emerged from a local experience, or in partnership with a deanery group or a parish representative. They were then extended to enable wider participation.

An integrated drama group

One such initiative was the integrated drama group, 'Hand in Hand' which was formed in spring 1994. For some years we had been running regular weekend retreats in the Diocese for adults with and without learning disabilities. As these developed, we had begun to use more dance and drama in our prayer and liturgy. Many people found this particularly helpful and the idea was floated to form a distinct group, which could further explore the use of movement and music to deepen and express faith. The group's two main aims were to discover Christ's presence in and among its members and in doing so, enrich their spiritual lives, and secondly, to share this with others in a prayerful way, using all types of drama.

Hand in Hand owes its creation to the vision and enthusiasm of many people, but especially to that of one particularly committed parish representative and catechist who helped lead the residential retreats and had long cherished a dream of combining spirituality and drama.

From the beginning the group was planned to be interdenominational, and for adults with and without learning disabilities on an equal basis. It currently has a regular membership of 28, of whom 16 have a learning disability. Most members are, however, Catholic and the initial hope of being truly interdenominational has yet to be realised. Members come from each of the three counties of the Diocese and, despite the travel difficulties posed by this, the group meets to rehearse monthly, and joins for a residential weekend annually.

Hand in Hand has a growing repertoire, which includes liturgical dance, hymns expressed through sign and gesture, and several dramatised Faith stories and mimes. It has been asked to prepare Gospel dramas and meditations for both Diocesan and local celebrations and in the years since its creation it has led worship and workshops for numerous parishes and groups. As members continue to work and pray together there is a growing sense of mutual commitment and belonging, and a deepening experience of prayer. Hand in Hand's activity and programme seems to be increasingly 'owned' and led by all of its members. It is clear from the enthusiasm shown that Hand in Hand has an important place not only in the lives of its members, but also in the lives of the increasing number of people brought into contact with it.

A conference for Christians

The same wish, to enable the voices of people to be heard in the church, provided the impetus in 1994 for a Conference for Christian Adults with Learning Disabilities. Its aim was simply to bring people together to talk about their experiences in the church, and to provide an opportunity to listen for those who do not have learning disabilities, yet who frequently make decisions on their behalf.

The Self Advocacy movement, encouraging people to 'speak for themselves', is some fifteen years old. In Britain, numerous groups have made great strides in raising awareness that people with learning disabilities have something to say about their own lives and should be listened to. But there seems to have been no similar exercises in the churches. In the four years since the Diocesan service had been in existence, wide contacts had been built up with families and people living in residential homes, so the time seemed right to include them in determining the direction of the services we offered.

A day conference was planned and advertised as widely as possible through church and social services networks, using symbolic as well as written material. A central, accessible venue was booked. The conference was interdenominational, and on the day, forty delegates took part, representing several different churches. The day was kept simple and uncluttered. There was a welcome and opening prayer, followed by sessions in small groups of four or five, assisted by facilitators who had attended earlier preparation meetings. The groups were asked to spend time getting to know one another, where they lived and where they went to church. They were then invited to talk about what they liked at church and made them happy, and what they did not like and made them sad. At the end of the day, groups reported back to the whole Conference, and we concluded with a time of prayer, led by delegates.

We are not used to really listening to people who have a disability in language and understanding. We need to allow a lot of time and attention if we are truly to hear what they are saying. What we heard at the conference was people's perception of themselves, in contrast to the perception that wider society or church might have of them. The way delegates saw themselves was not as recipients of care, but as adult members of their churches. They wanted to be involved and to contribute to the life of their church.

Their overall experience of the church seemed to be positive. Most found it much easier to talk about what they liked, rather than things they disliked. Their 'likes' included attending Mass or Sunday services, hymns, praying, bells, candles, and meeting and talking to the priest or vicar. Some mentioned having friends in the church, and the chance to go for coffee afterwards, though not all had this opportunity '*I don't go to the Church Hall because no-one takes me.*' Where delegates had a role in the church community it was clearly very important to them. These roles included serving at Mass, helping give out hymn books, singing in the choir, and locking up the church at the end of the day. When delegates talked about things which made them sad, not having a role came high on the list. Some said they would like to take the collection or offertory, to be a server, 'hold the chalice', or to 'hold the Bible for the priest when he reads it'. Their dislikes included 'people coughing loudly', 'babies crying when I'm listening' and 'when the readings are too fast'. It was striking that delegates found visual and symbolic aspects of liturgy helpful. Their difficulties, when they arose, often centred around words and listening, something to ponder on as we strive to make our church communities more inclusive.

Relationships were very important. Having friends in the church was mentioned in most groups. Great appreciation was expressed by those who took part in social or community building aspects of church, such as going on pilgrimage, joining a prayer group or attending a Diocesan celebration. One delegate told the conference that she lived in a residential home where people did not go to church, but that she wanted to live with people who prayed.

For those who attended, it was an important and enjoyable day. In many ways it felt similar to any other church meeting, in that delegates fell quickly into the structure of the day, group discussions frequently over-ran their time, and many of the more interesting discussions took place over coffee breaks! The wide range of delegates' likes and dislikes reflected almost exactly what could be expected from any mixed group from our congregations in the same age range. They were not unique to people with learning disabilities. Above all, what the conference heard was the repeated call for friendship, and the wish of so many delegates to be more involved and of some service in their church.

CONCLUSION

Building true community in our churches is a lifelong task. It is one that is shared by all members, both those with, as well as those without, learning disabilities. Much of our experience in the Diocese of Arundel and Brighton has felt like a discovery of something which has always been there, but perhaps until now, has been kept rather hidden. We are seeking approaches through which we can grow together. In doing so we are discovering unused gifts and opportunities, as well as deep pain. Above all, we are slowly and with difficulty, learning to listen to one another.

Biographical Note

Julia Granger became interested in working with people who have learning disabilities through reading the work of Jean Vanier, and through an experience of living in a Camphill Village Community during her social work training. When she qualified in 1981 she worked for five years with the Ark Housing Association as Co-ordinator of a community home for adults with learning disabilities in Edinburgh. She then became a manager with Mencap Homes Foundation in Sussex, establishing a number of small, staffed houses. Since

1990 she has been with the Catholic Children's Society in the Roman Catholic Diocese of Arundel and Brighton, developing pastoral support for children and adults with learning disabilities and their families.

11 SPRED
IN THE ARCHDIOCESE OF GLASGOW

Agnes Nelson

Introduction

A person doing a workshop on prayer once said something like this.

Imagine a tiny seed.

Imagine a rough gardener's hand with the seed cupped there.

Imagine how tenderly he lifts the seed and then makes a hole in the dark earth and carefully places the seed there.

Now the gardener covers the seed with the rich earth. The seed is enclosed in darkness but gradually life within it begins to stir and roots reach out for sustenance.

More and more the roots reach out until one day the hard earth above begins to soften and the shoot begins its journey towards the light.

More and more the roots anchor themselves and more and more bravely the shoot pierces its way through the dark soil towards the waiting sun.

Sometimes the shoot, no matter how hard it pushes cannot grow straight upwards but so great is its desire for sunlight that it finds a pathway round the obstacle. Eventually it breaks through the upper crust of the soil and strengthens in the fresh clear air.

In time it sprouts leaves and one day it bears the most beautiful fruit.

This image has deep meaning for me as I ponder and reflect on eleven years of SPRED in the Archdiocese of Glasgow. The seed is the SPRED method which I have studied for a year at Loyola University, Chicago and which I innocently planted in the dark soil of the Archdiocese. The roots are the management and support structures, and the training programmes that have been deeply embedded; the stones, the obstacles to growth; the shoot, the life of SPRED which grows and pulsates, '*the farmer knows not how*' (Mark 4:28); the leaves are the small faith communities scattered throughout the diocese and the fruits are the many signs of the Kingdom community.

The seed: Method

It may be at this point I should explain exactly what SPRED is and why this image of planting a new seed in a diocese is so apposite. SPRED is a catechetical programme for people of all ages who have intellectual disability. What makes SPRED revolutionary is the method it uses, a method that enables faith development. The model is not that of the classroom but the small faith community rather like the Right of Christian Initiation of Adults used in the Catholic Church today, but the difference is that the people concerned have mostly been considered ineducable in faith. In the world of catechetics, it has gradually been realised that God can be known intuitively as well as intellectually; that there is an affective way of thinking as well as a rational, and that there is a passive mode of consciousness as well as the active. This has given scope for creativity in the process of catechesis used with people who have developmental disability.

In Gilbert Osdick's book, *Catechesis for Liturgy*, he describes what is possibly the origin of this method. He calls it MYSTAGOGICAL CATECHESIS and it was the final stage in the initiation of adults into the early church. Prospective converts having had some initial formation, come to the Easter Vigil unaware of what will happen. They gather in darkness, they are immersed in water, anointed with fragrant oils, clothed in white robes, and jubilantly brought in torchlight procession for the first time into the midst of the assembly gathered for Eucharist. The meaning of these symbolic actions, or mysteries, was gradually reflected on during the period AFTER Easter as the new Christians continued to meet weekly with the Bishop. What is interesting about this ancient catechetical method is that the experience comes first then the reflection. We can call this SYMBOLIC CATECHESIS, a method that works extremely well with people who have intellectual disability because it draws on their life experiences, depends on intuition and, in general, touches on what has affected people and formed them. There is another part of a SPRED session called the LITURGICAL EVOCATION and this little jewel, using the same method, gives people the opportunity to ponder a liturgical event they have experienced - the gathering, the sign of peace, the offering of gifts, the breaking of bread, and sharing a cup. Evoking, remembering and pondering these experiences deepens awareness of God's presence and action, thus developing a more open spirit to God's saving touch in future celebrations. This method of catechesis is highly endorsed in Article 777 of the Code of Canon Law, which states that for people who have developmental disability, meaningful instruction on the sacraments is best AFTER the event.

If liturgical experiences are to be evoked, the Method is therefore presuming some kind of parish involvement, which brings us to the ultimate aim of SPRED. This is simply that people with a developmental disability take their rightful place in the parish community.

A Mustard seed will grow into a mustard tree; a pansy seed will grow into a pansy and what has most enabled the SPRED seed to take root is the vision of what the flowering plant will be: a community of believers who are mutually supportive; where the weak are seen to be 'blessed' having insights that are kept from the learned and the wise, and where resources and personnel are made available to nurture the faith-life of those who require specialised and skilled help. We see that at the kernel of this seed is Christ Himself; the Christ who is at the heart of all catechesis and who reveals Himself in His Word and sacraments and who is truly present when the community gathers together.

Roots: Foundation

> *Unless a grain falls on the ground and dies it remains only a single grain, but if it dies it yields a rich harvest* (John 12:25).

The seed contains in embryo all that is needed for the full flowering of the plant but unless strong roots are first formed, there will be little growth.

Since SPRED in the Archdiocese of Chicago has a life-span of 30 years it was fruitful to look at some of their documentation which identified good, solid foundations. Foremost among these was the formation of adult faith communities into which the people with developmental disabilities would be welcomed. Where these were weak or abandoned as part of the Method, the SPRED group did not last; it was founded on sand. In the 10 years of SPRED in the Archdiocese of Glasgow, the incubation, nurture, consolidation and on-going development of these adult faith communities has been the primary target of training programmes.

This method in SPRED offers a process of
=> reflection => action => reflection.

Inbuilt therefore is the assumption that catechists are trained in the skill of reflection. Symbolic catechesis works only if people believe in and reflect on their own life experiences. SPRED catechists must believe that the friends with disabilities have relationships and experiences that are worth recalling; that in the ordinary events of life God is present and speaking, comforting and affirming. The catechists can bring their friends to this Truth only if they see these revelations in their own lives. At every catechist preparation session, the helpers are invited to take time to ponder a question that evokes some past life experience. This 'space' for such a contemplative exercise repeated over the years, nurtures people, with the help of God's grace, in their ability to **BE** in faith. As 'maturity of faith' is, according to the General Catechetical Directory, 'the goal of all catechesis', we see that SPRED enhances the faith-life of catechists as well as that of the people with very specific pastoral needs.

There is another part of the reflective process called feedback where catechists evaluate what happened at the session with the disabled people. This is not just a remembering of events but an observation of faith. *"How was the goal of the session realised in me and how did I see others responding*?" For a new group, it is easy to fall into the trap of focusing on behaviour problems, funny stories or very superficially saying 'it was fine.' A more mature group, however, will notice what obstacles there were to the catechesis and what signs of growth were evident such as greater peace, more concentration, stillness and a response to God's Word. In summary, there was a realisation of a person's potential.

When people offer their services to SPRED, they usually want to do something for disabled people. Most of these people STAY in SPRED because they have experienced the dignity and giftedness of these same people. This is a kind of grappling with the mystery of God's revelation that it is those whom the world thinks most useless who are chosen to show up those who think they are everything. Gradually catechists who reflect on this mystery are led to a wisdom that enables them to recognise the witness proffered by the disabled. Once this has been grasped, it is a treasure hard to relinquish, so there is a high proportion of stability in Glasgow SPRED groups - another valuable and strong foundation. Putting such energy into personnel has been most rewarding as there are now Training Programmes in place for Directors at diocesan level; for area co-ordinators and Trainers at deanery level, and at the local level for leaders, helpers, activity catechists and parish chairpersons. This means others in the future can benefit from good strong roots which will provide for the continuance of SPRED.

Since the SPRED Method is so unique and unlike most of the catechetical experience to which people have been generally exposed, it was very important that from the earliest possible time observation facilities were made available. This would enable parents, educators, pastors and potential catechists to 'see' the Method with their own eyes and learn from the experience. It is the **skill** of catechesis, the **how** of catechesis and its **art form** that has to be passed on. There is a need to watch the artisan at work and the one-way viewing mirrors provide this opportunity. With this in place there is a TRAINING CENTRE for the whole diocese, a resource that ensures that high standards are maintained and proves that the implementation of the Method is possible.

SPRED operates through the formation of small faith communities but one of the dangers of small groups is that they become self-contained and cosy, finding all the support they need from within. SPRED's goal is integration into the parish community enabling those with intellectual disabilities to take their rightful place there, so it was important from the very beginning of SPRED's initiation into a new diocese that structures would be put in place to support this vision. Therefore, before even identifying a place for the TRAINING CENTRE it was important to ascertain if the parish in which the building was located was willing to support the work in raising awareness within its community of the spiritual rights of people with disabilities and welcoming them into its liturgical and social life. With this established, there was a model for all other SPRED centres throughout the diocese. It was inevitable that this way of working would be slow but this has proved in the long term to be the most effective. There are now 12 parishes in the Archdiocese of Glasgow where SPRED FAMILY LITURGY is a familiar part of the annual programme. These celebrations take place at one of the normal Sunday Services so that the parish grows in its awareness of its responsibilities and gradually appreciates being evangelised even as it reaches out to evangelise. The service, according to the Director of the Roman Missal, is prepared with the specific needs of its congregation in mind. These parish roots require much nourishment but produce many offshoots, a sure and steady foundation for the growth of SPRED.

The shoot and the leaves

The life of SPRED to which the strong foundations have given birth, lie in the 30 SPRED groups scattered throughout the Archdiocese and located in twelve parish centres. In each group there are ideally eight catechists, three of whom are trained for specialised leadership roles. Six of the catechists work on a one-to-one relationship with a person who has developmental disability. These groups meet regularly throughout the year, following the Programme set out in the Guidelines that are geared to the specific age group of the disabled people. The symbolic catechesis used in SPRED depends strongly on the life-experience of each member so catechists are trained and guided to make contact with families, group homes, schools or training centres. Thus one person with special pastoral needs is at the centre of a network of relationships bringing families, parishioners, catechists and drivers into closer communication and harmony. A story illustrates this well.

Pauline is aged 7 and she has a severe learning difficulty. Her mother is very loving but suffers from a terminal illness. She is a woman of faith and she is anxious that Pauline receive her First Holy Communion. Another mother tells her about SPRED and together they come to observe a SPRED session. At this time there is no group in the area Pauline could join but her mother persists in requesting a place. Eventually, the day comes when parents of a newly formed 6 to 10 age group are invited to come and see what SPRED offers, and to meet the catechists and drivers. For Mr and Mrs Tonner this was their first meeting with Paul and Sarah, the driver and assistant who would faithfully call for Pauline every second Tuesday and on those Sundays when there was a SPRED Family Mass. They also meet Mary, a mother of four boys, who would be Pauline's special friend and a confidant of Mrs Tonner over the next 3 years. Mary not only visited Pauline and her mother at home but often brought Pauline into her own family where she became one of them. In due course Pauline made her First Communion, to the delight of the extended family. Meanwhile, her illness was progressing and eventually Mrs Tonner died. The funeral Mass was for me a most moving occasion but it was also a witness of how relationships within SPRED go far beyond the group and affect the whole community. Every single catechist of the group was present at the mass together with Pauline's driver and assistant. Through the tears there was genuine compassion and concern, which evidenced a very sincere bond that has been formed with Mrs Tonner.

Reflecting on this experience of one seven-year old child who has brought so many lives together and who had inadvertently touched so many hearts, made me realise, '*the eloquence of God...embodied in those whom we tend to dismiss*' (Wadell, 1994). The network of people brought into this story is quite amazing; first Pauline's mother hears of SPRED from another mother; Pauline's mother then meets catechists and driver from the SPRED group. Pauline meets her special friend and is introduced to her family. All the catechists, the families of the disabled people, drivers and parishioners celebrate together, with Pauline and her extended family, the event of her first communion. This same community gathered many times for the Eucharist before coming together to support a family suffering bereavement. This is a most beautiful illustration of the Body of Christ, each one a different part and the weakest the most indispensable (1 Corinthians 12:22). Multiply this story 150 times (there are 150 disabled people in Glasgow SPRED), and we have some idea of the 'Life' pulsating throughout the diocese; the yeast that leavens the bread.

In 1987 SPRED in Glasgow had its first workshop for Liturgical Mime. It attracted only 5 people. In February 1996 there were 43 catechists at a similar workshop. What has brought this amazing response? I imagine it is the experience of leader catechists who have grown in awareness that their proclamation of God's Word is not always comprehended by those with learning difficulties. I know in my own group when I stand to read God's Word, three non-verbal, profoundly disabled teenagers watch me with great eagerness. I know they do not understand my words but they do interpret intuitively all my body language and facial expressions. I believe profoundly that God's Word is for all. Von Balthazar asserts this beautifully:

> *Since God Himself has created us in such a way that we must hear the Word of God if we are to be ourselves, he has also endowed us with the ability to hear it. Otherwise He would have contradicted Himself and would not be truth. This ability to hear the Word goes as deep in us as being itself; the Father created us as SPIRITUAL creatures and so we are 'hearers of the word'... the great fundamental fact is that God, in giving us faith, has also given us the ability to hear* (Balthazar, 1955).

Yet how are these intellectually impaired people to 'hear' God's Word if there are no preachers who proclaim it in a way they can comprehend? And, how are we to know that communication is happening? As leaders have become more confident in using liturgical mime they have experienced the response of stillness, of attentiveness, of awe, of mystery. Catechists have responded to a need and have discovered a new art form and that is why they come to the workshop; to practise and develop skill of speaking God's Word using liturgical mime. A choir spends many hours rehearsing for a performance so that the harmony and beauty of the sound will touch the spirit of the listeners. The experience of this beauty is beyond logic and the person knows that what is experienced cannot adequately be reduced to concepts or words. It is a pre-conceptual experience, to use the language of Denis Edwards (1984). Something similar happens as God's Word is communicated through gesture and movement. God transcends senses and intellect, coming close in this act of beauty.

The number of catechists in Glasgow who have come to appreciate this truth is a testimony to their fidelity to the reflective method of the SPRED programme that constantly leads people to evaluate the effectiveness of their sessions. At the heart of this reflection is the question, '*Are the friends being enabled to hear God's Word; to respond; to grow in relationship with God?*' People, who were at first shy about using liturgical gesture have become sensitive to a need and have responded. Their joy and enthusiasm has been tremendous.

Fruit

By their fruits you shall know them (Matthew 7:16).

The word 'fruit' in the Oxford dictionary is defined as the seed-containing part of the plant. The seed usually presupposes a flower so the fruits of ten years of SPRED in a diocese are hopefully **beautiful** and contain the element of **reproducibility**. Obviously this latter is a vital element if SPRED is to continue into the future and not be dependent on certain individuals.

In 1983 when I was searching for a Course in Religious Education for people with learning difficulties, none was available in the whole of Britain. Having studied SPRED at Loyola University, Chicago, it became clear to me that a similar pastoral course could be launched from Glasgow. Through dialogue with Loyola and St. Andrew's College, Glasgow, validation to a Certificate Course was awarded in 1988 and this upgraded to a SPRED Diploma in 1994. This, I believe, is the most beautiful and seed-bearing fruit of eleven years of SPRED in Glasgow. It is beautiful because sharing the vision of SPRED is like sharing something very precious, handing it over, knowing how it will enhance people's lives. Giving a gift to someone can be an extremely pleasant experience as the joy it will evoke in the receiver gives personal delight to the giver. Handing on the skills and expertise of SPRED, which will touch the lives of so many, is something akin to Paul's enthusiasm as he reached out to build the early Christian communities. There is a sense of privilege in passing on something that has been heard, touched, seen with our own eyes and watched.

The sharing, as for St John, makes 'our own joy complete' (1 John 1:4). When people complete the SPRED Diploma, they usually go back to their own diocese or region to plant the seed there. Within the seed is all the expertise and skill that will enable growth. A diocesan director has the competency to compile resources, train others and write materials. A director will also know to negotiate a contract, a salary, a budget and a plan of action as these all mark the church's acceptance and approval.

As SPRED has grown in the Archdiocese of Glasgow it has been necessary to respond to the ever-increasing demand on management and training with more qualified personnel. The modular nature of the diploma course has been helpful in responding to this need. Twelve catechists have been able to give 30 hours to Module 6, which is geared to develop skills in pastoral management at local and deanery level. Through this they become competent in organising, planning and communicating with a cluster of SPRED groups who share the same centre. Another group of six catechists are at present studying the philosophy of SPRED with a view to being involved in the ten-week initial training programme. Over the years about sixty catechists have undertaken the leadership module becoming grounded in the skills of listening, co-operating, collaborating and taking responsibility. In all these ways the seed of reproducibility is taking root and producing new shoots at local level.

Stones: the obstacles

We have looked at the SPRED seed with all its potential in embryo, at its strong roots in the training and formation programmes, at its pulsating life in the 30 SPRED groups located in 12 parishes and the rich fruit of the SPRED diploma course. What of the soil in which the seed was planted and what of the obstacles to growth? An extract from Catechesis in our Times will help in responding to this question.

> *As the 20th century draws to a close, the church is bidden by God and by events - each of them a call from him - to renew her trust in catechetical activity as the prime aspect of her mission. She is bidden to offer catechesis her best resources in people and energy without sparing effort, toil or material means in order to organise it better and to rain qualified personnel. This is no mere human calculation; it is an*

attitude of faith. And an attitude of faith always has reference to the faithfulness of God who never fails to   respond (Article 15).

In the Archdiocese of Glasgow there has been a great willingness at one level to respond to the implementation of SPRED but there have been great difficulties in trying to identify exactly in what departmental structure it belongs. In American dioceses, there is a well-established system of parish departments of Religious Education, so catechesis as a parish activity is not a new concept. In the West of Scotland, catechesis is part of the Religious Education programme in Catholic schools and preparation for the sacraments of Eucharist, Reconciliation and Confirmation is not primarily a parish concern. This means that financial and other resources are located within the school. SPRED is parish-based and it is concerned with faith-development beyond school age. Where then does SPRED find a home? For the past eleven years, there has been no identified line-management structure to foster catechesis. This has meant that SPRED has been 'out-on-a-limb', appreciated and approved - but isolated. This is a considerable obstacle in developing a sense of belonging within the diocese. The Bishops of England and Wales at its Conference in 1993 said,

We are convinced that the manner and style of relationships in the Church are part of the sign it gives, and for this reason we must develop patterns of collaborative ministry as a key feature of Church to come. We wish to encourage all these, men and women, who have been trying to implement and explore such new relationships, with all their difficulties and promises.

Such a statement gives hope of a brighter future and shows awareness of new-life struggling to give birth.

St Luke testifies in his writings (Acts 2:42-47; 4:32-35; 5:12-16) that the quality of the faith-life of the whole Christian community is the main instrument in the spreading of the gospel. Since the Vatican Council, perhaps for the first time since the early church **all** members are explicitly called into an evangelising partnership in which both clergy and laity are to have full, mature and mutually

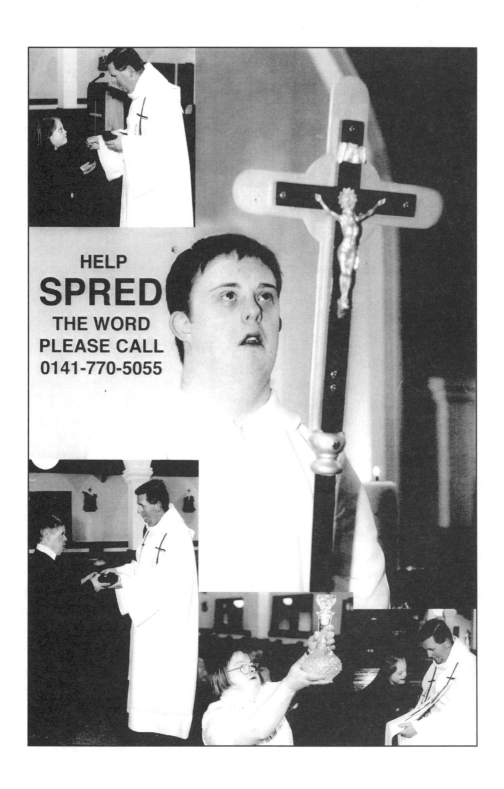

HELP
SPRED
THE WORD
PLEASE CALL
0141-770-5055

complementary roles. SPRED has trained 200 lay people to a level of considerable quality as catechists but perhaps the 'sign we give' is of laity and clergy not collaborating. There is a need for initiatives for dialogue from both sides so that the people with developmental disabilities and their families can be more fruitfully supported in their spiritual lives. Such development would enable these people to exercise their very gifted powers of evangelisation.

> *In SPRED, the group obviously does not put huge priority on books but on the space used. The space is the EDUCATIONAL environment. The space becomes a kind of chrysalis of the sacred, where the members are initiated into a way of relating, a way of being that will help them pass from being on the "outside" of the sacred to being on the "inside"; from being a stranger to being a member.* (Harrington, 1996).

This sacred space is essential if growth-in-faith is to be fostered. The ultimate sacred space in which we all share is the church building, God's people gathered in faith around the altar, the Word and the presider. As we have already seen, liturgy and catechises are intrinsically linked so the space where we gather for catechesis is vital to the success of the SPRED method. '*The church is bidden to offer catechesis her best resources*', says Catechesis in Our Times. The most vital resource for SPRED catechesis is 'ecclesial' space; sacred space that is a bridge between catechesis and liturgy. In SPRED's eleven years in the Archdiocese of Glasgow, the Training Centre (sacred space) has been rooms in a school. These have been adapted and arranged to accommodate the Method but there have been tremendous restrictions **on their use** and availability. Foremost among the difficulties is that this space is not seen as belonging to the church. It is not 'ecclesial' space. This could symbolise some kind of marginalisation of the very people in whom we are trying to foster a sense of belonging and of the diocesan staff who work with church and the disabled people. Together, they struggle to make real for themselves, the words of Paul Tournier, '*We feel we exist in so far as others accept, respect, welcome our existence, in so far as they prove it by listening to us, answering us and entering into dialogue with us*', (1969). Diocesan leaders need to be integrated into a place, into a community if they are to teach and lead effectively: people with learning disabilities need to be integrated into a community and 'experience' belonging.

Another vital resource for any organisation is finance. In a diocese SPRED finds itself competing for funds with many other respected and recognised charities. It has also to be remembered that in the West of Scotland, dioceses and parishes have not needed to provide finance for catechetics as this takes place in schools. People will readily assure you that there are many Trusts who will be only too willing to support 'the disabled'. However, SPRED is concerned with SPIRITUAL formation, with enabling people take their rightful place in the parish community and as my experience has grown, I have discovered that there are not many trusts which will contribute to an organisation having these goals. Secondly, the time involved in applying to trusts is amazingly excessive and requires someone skilled to be involved in this work on a regular basis, alternatively, the SPRED Director has to forsake the catechesis and the management of the programme. This lack of funding, especially for salaries (as growth demands more qualified personnel), is like a boulder blocking the growth of the shoot. Again Catechesis in our Times highlights the Bishop's responsibility.

> *Your principal role will be to bring about and maintain in your churches a real passion for catechesis, a passion embodied in pertinent and effective organisation, putting into operation the necessary personnel, means and equipment, and also* **financial resources** *(Article 63).*

Since the ministry of catechesis with people who have developmental disability has to be built from scratch, it is perhaps not surprising that so many difficulties exist. Central to this is what Pope John Paul II calls 'an attitude of faith'. It is only within the past 30 years that people with learning difficulties have seriously been considered educable in faith. Prior to this, terms such as 'little angels' and 'holy innocents' were often used and, although perhaps meant kindly, actually denied these people their humanness. Now we are saying such people can grow in faith if the correct method is used. However, the pragmatists are still looking for proof that growth in faith is really happening and are asking left-brain questions and wanting very rational answers. How do people "prove" that they know the Eucharistic bread is different? Can they give the theological answer? Is it not how we behave towards the "Holy Bread" that tells the heart story? Will people persist in asking children with learning difficulties for explanations that are beyond their language and cognitive ability? A person of faith will approach this whole question of readiness for sacraments by turning to the parents and the catechists and dialoguing with them, preparing with them and eventually celebrating with them.

In *All People Together* written in 1981 by the Catholic Bishops of England and Wales there is a whole section devoted to the mystery of disablement. This not only asserts that disabled people are full members of the human family but leads us to ponder the power of powerlessness drawing us into the pathos of God who reveals Himself/Herself where we least expect: '*hidden away in the lonely, shrouded in the harmless who disturb*' (Waddell, 1994). This insight highlights the faith-development required of the pastors and the catechists and they would do well to use the criteria for growth-in-faith (in themselves and in the disabled people) as set forth by St Paul in his letter to the Galatians; is there growth in love, in joy, in peace, patience, gentleness; in kindness, self-control and trustfulness?

CONCLUSION

In the Book of Isaiah we hear God speaking:

> *I will plant trees... cedars, myrtles, olive trees, the cypress, fir and pine...on **barren** land. Everyone will this see miracle and understand that it is God who did it*. (Isaiah 41:19).

In the Archdiocese of Glasgow the seed of SPRED has been planted and watered but it is God who provides the growth. The challenge for this Christian Community is to be a people of Faith; a people who recognise their need for support from **all** the other members; a people who recognise their incompleteness. Then the Lord will effect the miracle.

REFERENCES

Bishops of England and Wales: Report from the Working Party on Collaboration. (1995). *The Sign We Give.* Essex, England: Matthew James Publishers.

Edwards E. (1984). *Human Experience of God.* Dublin: Gill and Macmillan.

Harrington, T. (1996). *Space, an Opening to the Beyond.* Chicago: SPRED Newsletter Vol 37 No 1.

John Paul II. (1979). *Catechesis in Our Time.* Vatican Council II More Post Conciliar Documents. Northport, New York: Costello Publishing Company.

Tournie, P. (1969). *A Place for You.* New York: Harper and Row.

Von Balthasar, H. (1955). *Prayer.* San Francisco: Ignatius Press.

Waddell, P. (1994). Pondering the Anomaly of God's Love. In E. Foley (ed.), *Developmental Disabilities and SacramentalAccess.* Collegeville, Minnesota: The Liturgical Press.

Biographical Note

Sr Agnes Nelson is a qualified teacher who worked until 1983 in Dumbarton and Glasgow with children who have learning difficulties. Her interest in the spiritual formation of our brothers and sisters in the church who have learning disabilities led her in 1983 to train in symbolic catechesis in Loyola University, Chicago. On returning to Scotland in October 1984 she established Special Religious Education (SPRED) in the Archdiocese of Glasgow with St Mungo's parish as her base. Currently there are 30 SPRED groups serving twelve parishes and using about 220 catechists in the Archdiocese. It has given Sr Agnes great joy to see SPRED established in the Paisley (1990), Motherwell (1990), Edinburgh (1997) and Galloway (1998) dioceses.

12 FAITH AND LIGHT

Bob Brooke

Seacroft is a large council estate on the eastern edge of Leeds. It has a population of over 30,000 people, as many as a medium sized town. There is one large Anglican parish with five neighbourhood churches served by a team of clergy, there are two Catholic parishes and three smaller churches - Methodist, Baptist and Congregational.

The Seacroft Faith and Light community meets once a month on a Sunday afternoon. It is supported by Churches Together in Seacroft and welcomes people with learning disabilities, other members of their families and those who want to become their friends. Most of the regular members are Catholic or Anglican but some have no particular church background. The group alternates its meetings between St Luke's Anglican Church and Our Lady of Good Counsel Catholic Church. This is one way of saying, that this community does not belong to any particular church or denomination, but is for everybody whatever church they belong to.

A FAITH AND LIGHT MEETING

At our regular monthly meetings when everyone has arrived, we sit in a circle, welcome everybody, especially anyone who is new, then begin with a song - usually a lively, familiar song of praise to God, sometimes with people playing tambourines or small drums or other percussion instruments and everybody else clapping their hands. The theme of our worship is introduced and then we sometimes split into small groups perhaps to prepare some art or rehearse some drama. When we come back into the circle we sing another song and then the table is prepared. Someone will bring our special tablecloth, which has on it the outline of the hands of everybody in our community. Someone else will bring the Bible, then the candles, a picture of Jesus, on the Cross, or at the Last Supper with his disciples, and sometimes some flowers.

We continue with our liturgy by confessing our sins to God and hearing that he forgives us, then we share the peace with each other. The story from the Bible may then be presented, usually in a visual, dramatic, participatory way. Sometimes everybody has a part to play for example, as a member of the crowd or being the noise of the wind or a storm. Later we have our time of prayer, when whoever wants to pray is encouraged to do so. Recently we have been growing more confident and relaxed about praying. Some of our members can and will pray quite clearly and audibly for someone or something they are concerned about, or they will ask the rest of us to pray for them if they are feeling unwell or anxious about anything. Others need a bit of help putting into words prayers which come from the heart. Sometimes when we are praying for people who are very ill or who have died we open up old wounds in many of our members, but we are finding ways of accepting and supporting each other as we offer together our tears and sadness and concerns to God as well as our joys and prayers of thanksgiving. We often use candles to help people to focus their prayers and take as much time as people need so nobody feels too hurried. We usually conclude our prayers by joining hands and saying the "*Our Father*" together. Our worship ends with another song of praise and thanksgiving.

We try to make our worship as visual and as participatory as possible. We often use gestures and signing with our hands in our prayers and in our singing. Sometimes we incorporate into our worship some simple activity where everybody contributes something - say a candle, a little picture, a pebble, a small cross or a flower which we each bring and put together either to make something bigger such as one big cross or simply to place in front of the cross or the big candle which represents Jesus in our midst. After our worship we share news, remember people's birthdays, take part in a raffle and then conclude our time together with a shared meal. Everybody is encouraged to bring some food to share so there's usually a great pile of sandwiches, sausage rolls and cakes which all disappear very quickly.

MORE THAN A MONTHLY MEETING

Most of the people with learning disabilities who are members of the Seacroft Faith and Light community live apart from their families in group homes or hostels or in one or two instances live independently in their own flats. Some of them have little or no contact with other members of their families. The welcome they receive and the friends they have made in Faith and Light have been particularly important for them. Their involvement has helped them grow in trust and confidence, knowing that Faith and Light is somewhere they feel accepted, welcome and safe.

In a Faith and Light community people with learning disabilities, other family members and friends all find themselves together in a safe protected place where everything proceeds at the pace of the person with learning disabilities. We try not to attempt anything that will be beyond the grasp of the people with learning disabilities in our community. We find ourselves re-examining the Gospel stories – the means by which the basics of our faith are communicated, to try to express these truths in ways that are real and immediate to the people with learning disabilities. This provides an opportunity for everyone however simple or sophisticated to re-discover these truths and these stories in a new and refreshing way.

Faith and Light has provided a way into the church for some people with learning disabilities and their families, and helped them feel confident and comfortable in Christian worship. Faith and Light is much more than a kind of club which just meets once a month, it aims to be a community where all who come have a place and can make a valued contribution as well as receive what they need. This means that relationships continue beyond the monthly meetings. We visit each other, get to know each other's domestic situations; we share meals and outings with each other as well as coming together once a month for our meeting.

In many communities parents play a much bigger part than they do in Seacroft and the opportunity for them to meet together, share their stories and support each other in a context of acceptance and prayer has been very important.

The Charter and Constitution of Faith and Light suggest that a Faith and Light community should consist of at least 10 and no more than 50 people one third of whom will be people with learning disabilities, one third parents or other family members, and one third those who want to become their friends; but each community is different and develops in a way that is appropriate to its situation.

HOW FAITH AND LIGHT BEGAN

Faith and Light has become a worldwide family. At the time of writing there are around 1,300 Faith and Light communities in about 70 different countries meeting at least once a month, but it began in a very small way with just one family. In 1968 a French couple Camille and Gérard wanted to take their two sons Loïc and Thaddée who have profound learning disabilities with them on their local diocesan pilgrimage to Lourdes. However, it was made clear to them that they would not be welcome. The were told that their two sons were "too disabled", "would not be able to understand" and "would upset everybody". The family were still determined to go to Lourdes and so made their own arrangements and went by themselves. However, they were not made to feel welcome. In the hotel they were told, "Your meals will be served in your rooms, we don't want other people to be disturbed by seeing your sons." In the streets and at the grotto they overheard people saying, "Children like that should be kept at home." People looked away or crossed the street when they saw them coming. It was a terrible experience for the whole family.

Camille and Gérard went and told their story to Jean Vanier who had started the first l'Arche community a few years before and to Marie-Hélène Mathieu who was the Director of a national Catholic agency for disabled people in Paris. Out of this came the idea of a pilgrimage in which people with learning disabilities would be at the centre to help the Church be more aware that they are children of God with the same spiritual needs and gifts as other people. Parents would be invited to take part too, but it was important that they should not be left to care for their sons and daughters on their own so friends, especially young people were to be invited to take part in this pilgrimage. It took three years to prepare. The pilgrimage was not going to be a gathering of individuals but of already formed small communities of people with learning disabilities, their families and friends who would meet together in their home towns before sitting off to go on the pilgrimage together. It would be called Faith and Light.

On April 9th 1971 there were 12,000 Faith and Light pilgrims in Lourdes, 4,000 of them were people with learning disabilities. They had come from 15 countries and in Lourdes they experienced three days of indescribable peace and joy. The people of Lourdes who in anticipation of this invasion of disabled people had pulled down the shutters of their shops gradually moved from fear to surprise to a sort of astonished welcome. There was a real outpouring of the Holy Spirit and an extraordinary unity created between all those who took part so that on the last day people were saying, "It can't end here!" Jean Vanier told the pilgrims to, "Go home and do whatever the Holy Spirit inspires you to do - find ways to create loving communities around people with learning disabilities."

AN INTERNATIONAL FAMILY

Gradually, little Faith and Light communities began to develop in different towns and cities and in different countries bringing together people with learning disabilities, their parents and friends accompanied usually by a priest or minister whose role was to help the community understand more about the gift and the special mysterious beauty of the person with the learning disability.

In 1981 a tenth anniversary pilgrimage was made again to Lourdes involving pilgrims from Faith and Light communities in 27 countries. At Easter 1991 the movement's ecumenical vocation was deepened by a pilgrimage to Lourdes in which Faith and Light members from different Christian denominations from 63 countries came together to pray, "Father make us one, that the world might believe."

ECUMENISM

Faith and Light began within the Roman Catholic Church, although a number of Protestants did take part in the first pilgrimage in 1971. As the Movement

spread to countries where the majority of Christians are not Roman Catholic, Faith and Light communities began to spring up in other churches. In Switzerland, the UK, Scandinavia, Germany and various parts of Africa communities have come into existence rooted in various Protestant churches and in the Middle East and some parts of Eastern Europe some Faith and Light communities have begun in Orthodox Churches. Some communities like the one in Seacroft bring together members who belong to various Christian denominations. Sometimes through Faith and Light people with learning disabilities have brought together in prayer and fellowship people of different traditions who would not otherwise have come together.

In England some communities are based in Anglican or Methodist churches as well as Roman Catholic and others bring together Christians from different denominations. Most Faith and Light communities in Scotland have a mixture of people from different churches.

FAITH AND LIGHT IN THE UK AND IRELAND

Ireland, Scotland and Wales each have their own national organisation and England is divided into two autonomous areas North and South. Retreats, holidays, pilgrimages and formation sessions for leaders and chaplains are often arranged nationally. In October 1996, the English communities travelled to Walsingham to join in an ecumenical pilgrimage to mark the 25th anniversary of the founding of the Movement. Various links have been established with Faith and Light communities in other countries. Communities in Ireland, the UK and Scandinavian countries have a special relationship with communities in West and Southern Africa, and exchange information and support each other in prayer and with finance. Some individual communities have developed links with communities in other countries. The communities in Leeds for example have got to know and have arranged exchange visits with members of communities around the French city of Lille with which Leeds is twinned.

TELLING STORIES

Many people with learning disabilities have become cut off from their cultural and religious roots. They may have never heard the Gospel stories and may need to hear them time and time again before they grasp the meaning they have for them. If the stories they have heard all their lives have confirmed them in their identity as those who are worthless and to be rejected, left out of the mainstream of life, they will not be able to hear the Gospel stories or at least will not see that they are for them.

Just as it is important to re-tell the Gospel stories at our Faith and Light meetings, so it is important for us to know the story of Faith and Light and to hear that we are part of the movement which began with Camille and Gérard, their two sons, and their friends Jean Vanier and Marie-Hélène. The story of how Faith and Light began and has spread all over the world is a story of how the experience and pain of rejection was coped with and overcome. It is a story about our identity as Faith and Light, about who we are and it is a story that is re-lived time and time again in our Faith and Light communities. Many people who perhaps have experienced rejection or have a low opinion of themselves because of what the world at large says about them have found in their Faith and Light community a place where they know they are accepted and loved and where they can be themselves and grow in confidence, in self acceptance and self esteem.

As the rest of us who are members of Faith and Light communities become aware of the vulnerability of our friends with learning disabilities and their need for love, we too are set free to recognise and acknowledge our own needs for love and our own vulnerability As we see our friends relaxing and having a good time at our Faith and Light meetings we begin to relax and have a good time too.

The Feast of the Presentation of Christ or Candlemas (2nd February) has become a very special time for Faith and Light. Communities that are near enough to each other come together to celebrate this festival. We hear again and often act out the story of the parents Mary and Joseph bringing their special child to the Temple and meeting Simeon and Anna, friends who see who Jesus is - see him as a special gift from God. That story has become very important for us in Faith and Light. It has become part of our identity. Often when we gather at that time of year to celebrate what we call the Feast of Light, we bless and give to each other candles which are then taken back to be lit and used at our community meetings throughout the year. At these celebrations we often renew our commitment to each other and to God. When the Faith and Light communities in West and North Yorkshire come together for the Feast of Light we sometimes give each person a snowdrop - the first tiny flower to appear from the frozen earth of winter - a little sign of hope and of new life.

Biographical Note

Bob Brooke is an Anglican Priest, Chaplain for People with Learning Disabilities in the Anglican Diocese of Ripon. He is Chaplain to the Seacroft Faith and Light community and since 1992 has been convenor of the Movement's Ecumenical Commission.